AN ALBAN INSTITUTE PUBLICATION

Saying Goodbye

A TIME OF GROWTH

FOR CONGREGATIONS

AND PASTORS

Edward A. White

Handwritten inscription:

Bo Bailey
God Bless You,
Keep You
and Use You
in your
Ministry
AB Hicks, Phd
9/2000

50¢

Mail to
LeRoy Bailey
[illegible]

D0168152

Library of Congress Catalog Number 89-82321
ISBN #1-56699-037-8

To Good Shepherd Faith Presbyterian Church
and to National Capital Presbytery
who said Goodbye with elegance

CONTENTS

ACKNOWLEDGMENTS

"Should I Leave?" by Warner White first appeared in *Action Information*, Volume XII, No.1, January–February 1986.

"How Long Should a Pastor Stay" by John Esau first appeared in the *Mennonite Weekly Review*, April 20, 1989. Dr. Esau is Director of Ministerial Leadership Services, General Conference, Mennonite Church.

"Saying Goodbye: A Time of Personal Growth" was written by Craig Williams, a Presbyterian pastor in Trabuco Canyon, California

"On Living the Leaving," written by Chandler Gilbert, describes his journey through retirement from a United Church of Christ congregation in Concord, Massachusetts.

"Reflections on Ending Ministry in a Congregation" by Ingram C. Parmley first appeared in *Action Information*, Volume XI, No. 5, September–October 1985.

"The Pastor Says Goodbye" by Anthony Plathe first appeared in *Action Information*, Volume XII, No. 6, November–December 1986.

"Saying Goodbye to My Parish" by D. Hugh Peniston first appeared in *Action Information*, Vol. VI, No. 2, April 1980, pp. 8–10.

"How Do We Say Goodbye?" by Alice Martin first appeared in *Action Information*, Vol. III, No. 1, March 1977, p. 7.

"When a Church Dies" by Daphne Burt first appeared in *Action Information*, Volume XIV, No. 5, September–October 1988.

"A Service for the Ending of a Pastoral Relationship" was adapted by Edward A. White for ecumenical use from an Episcopal order of service.

"A Litany for the Closure of a Ministry" was adapted by Edward A. White for ecumenical use from an Episcopal order of service.

"Just When You Appreciate Them Most . . . They Leave Home" was written by Pat Engelmann of the University United Methodist Church in East Lansing, Michigan.

"At Home in the Wilderness: A Sermon on Saying Goodbye" was written by Edward A. White.

"What to Do Until the Preacher Comes: A Sermon for the Transi- · tion Time in the Life of a Congregation" was written by Edward A. White.

"From the Pastor's Desk" was written by Ralph Johnson of the Newcastle Presbyterian Church in Newcastle, Delaware on the occasion of his retirement after 26 years in the parish.

"My Friend, the Former Pastor" by Joan Mabon first appeared in *Action Information*, Vol. VI, No. 2, April 1980, pp. 6–7.

"Leaving the Pastorate: Staying in Town" by Rod L. Reinecke first appeared in *Action Information*, Vol. XIII, No. 5, September–October 1987, p. 11.

"Dear Henry" was written by John Esau, Director of Ministerial Services of the Mennonite Church.

Saying "Hello!" and Saying "Goodbye!" Are the Two Major Learning Tasks All Humans Need to Accomplish.[1]

This is a book about saying "goodbye!"

How do a congregation and pastor end a relationship gracefully in a manner that enables them to:

1. Learn from and affirm the journey they have shared together?

2. Deal with their feelings about saying goodbye so as to become free to enter wholeheartedly into the next chapter of their respective separate journeys?

3. Experience the Gospel dimensions of death and resurrection as they deal with endings and new beginnings?

4. Avoid doing each other harm?

Why Are Goodbyes Important?

The transitions in our lives are often the most significant periods of growth. Leaving the womb, leaving home, going to college, one's first job, getting married, having children, receiving a promotion or a transfer, losing a loved one, facing suffering and death—these are the moments when we are stretched and challenged in new ways. The established patterns of life are overturned and we must find new ways to cope. The predictability of life is replaced by uncertainty. We experience vulnerability, fear, and exhilaration.

If we make the transition successfully we experience a new

sense of capacity for living, a new sense of maturity and self-worth. We discover the mystery and wonder that by God's grace we can surrender the old and embrace the new.

On the other hand, if we fail in these transitions there may come a diminished sense of self-worth and capacity for living; we experience impotence and failure. Often we are tempted to blame others for our pain and to act in ways that are destructive to them and/or ourselves. We may remain unhappily in the old and familiar, or enter the new with hostility and distrust. How many pastors do you know who:

1. *Stayed too long in one church because for one reason or another they could not make a transition?* I know cases where a pastor cost the congregation half its membership by getting "stuck" in this way.

2. *Blamed their people for their need to move, thereby laying a guilt trip on the congregation?* Destructive departures can take years to heal. I filled the pulpit on the Sunday after a pastor had left. When I arrived I was told that the pastor in his final sermon the Sunday before had vehemently castigated individuals by name from the pulpit. The congregation was in a state of shock and "bleeding" profusely. I did not preach a sermon that Sunday. I simply came down out of the pulpit and invited folks to share their pain. For the next hour there was a ventilating that began the long slow process of recovery from a deep wound that had been inflicted in just twenty minutes by a pastor who had not learned how to say goodbye.

3. *Created unhealthy dependencies in their congregation, making it difficult for the church to cope well after their departure?* This is the workaholic pastor who needs to "do it all" himself or herself, thus casting the congregation in the passive spectator role. It's like the parent whose personal needs will not allow their child to grow up. It is difficult for an unhealthy relationship to result in a healthy goodbye.

4. *Kept trying to hang on or come back after they had resigned in a manner that created problems for the congregation and the successor* (this is a symptom of 3)? When a particular pastor and particular people have become indispensable to each other, where is God in all of this?

5. *Acted heroic and was completely cheerful throughout the departure process, not revealing any feelings of grief, pain, or anxiety?* These are the "Richard Cory's of the cloth" who have learned

that no one can be self-sufficient or invulnerable except the preacher. Such a witness will not encourage the congregation to own and deal with its own pain and grief.

6. *Fled in haste and never gave the congregation a chance to say goodbye or to experience closure?* I have heard of one such pastor whose successor had great difficulty making pastoral contact with the congregation. The successor finally figured out the problem: the members had not yet said goodbye to the former pastor. So a year later he requested the former pastor to return for a farewell party. After that things went well.

7. *Carried the unresolved pain of conflicts in the previous parish into the entry process with a new congregation, thereby contaminating the developing relationships right at the outset?* If the first eighteen months of a pastorate is the "formative period," one can be sure that this kind of start-up will not be fruitful.

All of these are destructive ways of dealing with the trauma of transition from one parish to another. They do great harm to pastors and to people. Perhaps most tragic is the fact that the opportunities for spiritual and emotional growth of both pastor and people are blocked.

How We Say Goodbye Makes All the Difference in the World!

This issue has been critical during my thirty-three years of ministry in the Presbyterian Church—U.S.A.

When I left my first parish it required two years to deal with the pain of leaving a much loved congregation.

During almost twenty-two years on a Presbytery staff and as a Presbytery Executive I spent countless hours repairing the damage of destructive goodbyes to both congregations and pastors.

At the end of that ministry, perhaps because of lessons learned, I experienced a most rewarding closure at the hands of National Capital Presbytery. I left feeling loved and supported and with a sense of completion that has launched me into a new chapter in life.

This anthology addresses the following questions:

- How does a pastor know when it's time to leave?
- How does one say goodbye in a manner that enhances the future of both pastor and people?

- How can saying "goodbye" become an occasion for spiritual growth?
- How do we express closure in the context of worship?
- What special circumstances can affect the way we say goodbye?
- What are the ethics of the relationship after we've said goodbye?

NOTE

1. Attributed to John Hughes.

PART I

How Does a Pastor Know When It's Time to Leave?

A pastor is a leader. It is the leader's responsibility to know when it's time to leave. If the pastor waits until the people conclude that it's time for him or her to leave, then the pastor has become the follower.

Robert K. Greenleaf says that a leader needs to "have *a sense for the unknowable* and be able to *foresee the unforeseeable.*"[1] He even describes the failure to anticipate the future as an ethical failure.

During my twenty-one years with National Capital Presbytery I saw ninety-one ministers leave their congregations unhappily. Frequently the tragedy was simply that the pastor did not sense when it was the right time to leave.

When pastors stay too long the result is harmful both for them and the congregation. What does a congregation do when a pastor reaches age sixty, ceases to really invest in the ministry, and refuses to leave? To force the pastor out involves a heavy burden of guilt for the congregation. To simply endure several years of stagnant ministry invariably results in severe attrition and loss of morale. A pastor who stays too long is betraying a trust.

In "Should I Leave?" Warner White offers some excellent principles for monitoring one's tenure. He is speaking mainly to situations where there is conflict surrounding the leadership of the pastor. The mere presence of conflict is not a reason to leave. In some cases it may be a reason to stay. Who is unhappy and why? Warner advises us to "listen to the heart of the congregation," i.e., those people who make up the faithful leadership core.

There may be times, however, when a pastor should initiate a move even when there is no present conflict. Sometimes it's desirable to leave when the congregation is healthy and doing well. In "How Long Should a Pastor Stay?" John Esau suggests some of the practical considerations that should enter into the decision about making a move.

NOTE

1. Robert K. Greenleaf, *Servant Leadership* (Cambridge, MA: Center for Applied Studies, 1970, p. 22).

Should I Leave?
A Letter from One Priest to Another

by Warner White

Dear Harry,

I've been mulling over our phone conversation and I've decided to write you a letter. I want to speak as clearly, as systematically, and as theologically as I can to the question you're asking yourself, "Should I leave my parish? Should I be seeking a new rectorship?"

What struck me most was your telling the vestry at the time you were called to be rector, "I do not want ever to be the center of controversy the way Father Jones was, and if the time arrives that I am, I will leave." I believe I understand your reasons. The parish was split apart over Father Jones. It appeared to you very likely that he should have left earlier, on his own, without being pressured into going. You vowed to yourself that you would never be the source of such discord. Today it seems that you are. You find yourself attacked by some parishioners and defended by others. You say to yourself, "Here it is. Just what I feared. I want no part of it. I will leave."

We talked well together the other day, you and I, because we trust each other, because despite your newness in the priesthood you are a mature man with much experience of human nature, and because you are also humble and want to "pick my brains," to learn from my years of experience. So here goes. Let me tell you the principles of judgment I have come to and the experience that led me to them.

Principle 1. *You are a symbol to your congregation.*

For your congregation you are not just Harry Woolman. You are *The Priest.*[1] You are a walking image of something deep in the human soul. To understand what is going on in a parish you must be very clear about the difference between the rector as a person (you, Harry) and you as symbol-priest.

For example, from time to time I call on someone in the hospital who is from out of town. Almost always they greet me with warmth and trust. I do very simple things for them. I enquire about their health. We talk a little. I say a prayer. I anoint them—the ordinary things that clergy do. Yet they often react with immense gratitude and admiration for me. I swell inside. I have a sense of great power, of being bigger than life for them. I also have a sense of unreality. I'm just me. What I've done is very ordinary, and yet they are reacting as if it were very extraordinary.

What has happened? Is it me, Bill Hampton, they are reacting to? I think not, for the reaction is far out of proportion to what I in my real personhood have done. No. They are reacting to *The Priest*. What they are seeing is not me, but me-as-symbol. I'm feeling larger than life because this person is seeing me as larger than life. To be a priest is to be singled out to be for others a symbol of divine power and caring. Priesthood is not a property belonging to you or me; it is a clothing we put on for others.

After you have been in a parish for a while, and parishioners begin to see your humanity as well as your priesthood, you can begin to notice how at times they see other clergy differently from the way they see you. For example, have you ever felt a twinge of jealousy at the fuss and bother, the seeming excess of regard, the adoration almost, you perceive in lay persons as they prepare for the bishop's visitation? How do you react to the admiration shown by lay persons for the visiting priest who has just said something you've been trying to tell them for years? I find myself thinking, "I know him. He's just an ordinary guy like me. Why are they turning such cartwheels? They don't do that for me!" They are seeing *The Priest* where you and I see just another of our fellows.

From time to time parents tell me in laughter of ways in which their children confuse me with God or with Jesus. The children hear that I'm going on vacation and they ask their parents if there will be church, since "God is going away."

We laugh. Isn't that just like children! But down deep it's also like adults! The priest-symbol triggers deep hopes and fears and longings. Clothed in priesthood, you and I evoke the longing for a loving father, for the perfectly caring one who will make things all right. We evoke fears of wrath, of failing to please. We evoke deep hopes of being understood and valued by one who really matters.

Principle 2. *The priest is always the center of controversy in a parish.*

In a parish the priest is not only a symbol. The priest is also a human being. The priest's mere humanity shows. The tension between these two factors, the priest as symbol and the priest as human being, is probably the most difficult problem for priests and parishes to live with. It means that at all times there are disappointed parishioners, parishioners who long deeply for *The Priest*, for the larger-than-life holy one of God who will rescue them and care for them—and what they find instead is Harry Woolman or Bill Hampton. Make no mistake. The large gap between *The Priest* and our personal reality is a serious scandal to many persons. They hope for much more than we are able to be for them, and their disappointment is deep.

Some parishioners never get over their disappointment. They become deeply angry at us and remain so. I have found such anger and disappointment very difficult to deal with. I have sometimes been tempted to leave a parish in order to escape it. But that's a mistake. Only if your judgment is that your weaknesses are so severe as to invalidate your sense of call, and only if your judgment is confirmed by observers who care for you, should this be a reason for leaving.

Principle 3. *Pay attention to the character of the pastoral bond.*

When you and I accept a call to a parish, we and our parishioners commit ourselves to a pastoral relation. We exchange vows in a ceremony much like a wedding.

That step establishes the pastoral relation, but it is only the beginning. From that moment on what matters is the process of *bonding* between priest and parish. What matters is the way in which priest and parish become attached to one another in spirit, emotion, and behavioral pattern. The priest's pastoral task in the early years is the building and nurturing of that pastoral bond.

There are several elements in the pastoral bond—trust, caring, regard, power, centering, and the like. In a healthy process of bonding these elements go through various stages until the bond is established. I shall discuss three of them—regard, power, and centering.

The marriage encounter movement teaches that marriages go through three stages—illusion, disillusion, and realistic love. The illusion stage is the honeymoon stage, the stage in which the partners see each other through rosy glasses, in which the partners are on their best behavior. She is wonderful! Everything I ever dreamed of! She is the answer to all my longings ... Thus I see her more in terms of my own longings than in terms of her reality.

Then comes disillusion. I begin to see her humanity, and I am disappointed. This is a very painful stage in which the partners can be very cruel. All too often they become so disillusioned they seek divorce. But if all goes well, the partners begin not only to see each other realistically, but to accept and respect each other as they are. When this happens the partners find great joy. Now she loves me for who I am! Now I love her for who she is! We love the real person, not the illusion. Now I am able to reveal myself to her without fear of losing her, and she is able to reveal herself to me.

I would expect the honeymoon between priest and parish to last a year or two, disillusionment to last three or four years, and realistic love to arrive thereafter. Any decision about leaving or staying must take into account the stage of the bonding process. Where are you in that process? What should be happening at the present time?

These stages can be applied to the bonding elements of regard and power.

Principle 4. *A healthy bonding process goes through three stages of regard—adoration, disappointment, and respect.*

"Adoration" is a very powerful word to use for the regard shown a priest at the beginning of the pastoral relation. Perhaps it is too strong. I choose it, nevertheless, because it expresses the particular nature of the "rosy glasses" with which the priest is viewed in the honeymoon stage.

I once heard a priest describe how he was greeted in his new parish as "the messiah," "the one who was going to set all things right." "And the trouble was," the priest added, "I believed it! I thought I really was going to do all those things." He went on to describe his own disillusionment with himself, as well as the disillusionment of his parish, when they discovered that he couldn't do everything they had hoped for.

"Adoration" suggests, accurately I believe, that the priest is viewed in divine terms. The priest-symbol is superhuman. When we begin a new ministry that's where we begin. Larger than life hopes and longings are stirred up and are focussed on us by parishioners. And we, too, are likely to have larger-than-life fantasies of what we will accomplish, of adoring crowds coming to hear us preach, of large numbers of converts through our ministry, of great social action programs being carried out, and the like. This is especially true early in our priesthood.

Then, of course, comes disappointment. We and our parishioners become painfully aware of our mere humanity. We and they are faced with the necessity of accepting a merely human rector, instead of a messiah. If that task is successfully completed, and both priest and parish move on to the stage of respect, in which the priest respects himself or herself, and in which the parish respects the priest in that priest's humanity, a healthy bond of regard is established.

I do not believe that *The Priest* ever vanishes, however. Even when you and I are known as the human beings we are, we remain, somehow, still the image of *The Priest*. We are still walking symbols of God's care and love for his people. In a healthy pastoral bond the tension between humanity and *The Priest* is resolved, not by banishing *The Priest*, but by accepting the human being.

I have come to understand the meaning of clerical dress and of vestments in this fashion. These special forms of clothing are a concrete sign that the person who wears them is functioning as a symbol, even though he be merely Harry Woolman or Bill Hampton.

Notice that in the progression from adoration, through disappointment, to respect, there is also a progression in perception. At first parishioners know little about the rector as person. They see the rector as priest-symbol. Later, if all goes well, they are able to perceive symbol and real person in harmony. They respect the person who plays the symbol and they accept that person's offering of the symbol to them.

I speculate that in many of those cases where parishioners become stuck in the stage of disillusion, the rector as real person is never perceived. Instead the rector becomes the symbol of antichrist. "We thought he was the messiah, but he is just the opposite!" The rector becomes the symbol of betrayal at the most profound level.

Just as "adoration" may seem too strong a term for positive regard at the beginning of a new ministry, so "antichrist" may seem too strong a term for the negative aspect. And perhaps it is. Yet I have received letters from disillusioned parishioners couched in negative language so strong as to suggest depths of evil far beyond my limited capacities!

In these cases parishioners flip the superhuman coin. They flip from perceiving the rector as beneficently superhuman to seeing the rector as maleficently superhuman. They never perceive him or her as truly human at all.

Principle 5. *A healthy bonding process goes through stages of power settlement.*

Group formation theory distinguishes three stages in power settlement—dependence, counterdependence, and interdependence. In a new group the members at first wait upon the designated leader to give direction. They depend upon the leader to get things going. Later they begin to see faults in the leader's performance and begin to rebel against the leader. Finally, group and leader develop patterns by which they depend upon each other.

These stages can be distinguished in the process of bonding between priest and parish. At first parishioners wait to see what direction the new rector will take. They look for clues to the new rector's intentions, and their general tendency is to cooperate. Later they begin to find fault, and finally they work out a pattern of decision making that is a balance of the forces within the parish.

Principle 6. *The bonding agenda is set by the character of the previous pastoral relations of the parish and of the priest.*

It is well known that parishes tend to call priests as rector in reaction to the character of the previous rector. If the previous rector focussed on social action and neglected spiritual life, the parish is likely to look for the same in the new rector if they were happy with the previous rector and to look for the opposite if they were unhappy. This sets the parish's agenda with the new priest.

Similarly, the priest seeks to establish the same or different characteristics in the new pastoral relation in accordance with the priest's previous experience. This sets the priest's agenda with the new parish.

So two agendas set by past experience come together to form the details of what must be worked through in the bonding process. In my present parish I am very conscious that parishioners have been testing me on matters made important to them by their experience with my predecessor. I noticed that in the early months of our relationship they tended to interpret my actions in accordance with the character of my predecessor. I am also conscious that I have been looking for the likenesses and differences between this parish and my previous parish. *The bonding process is not complete until the past agendas have been dropped, and new agendas based on present realities have been adopted.*

You must ask yourself about the present controversy surrounding you. "What agenda is it? Is this controversy a leftover from my predecessor, or does it realistically concern me and this parish?"

Principle 7. *Of special importance for the new rector are the bonding agendas of your predecessor's in-group and out-group.*

Your predecessor undoubtedly had an in-group, a group of people to whom he was especially close and who felt supported by him, persons whose needs he met in a way satisfying to them. He also had an out-group, people unhappy with him in various ways, who felt distant from him. When a new rector arrives each group has a special agenda. The in-group hopes that they will have the same relationship with the new rector, and the out-group hopes for something better. The in-group will seek to continue the set patterns. The out-group will seek to change them.

Chances are that neither group will be completely satisfied. The new rector is a different person and will not satisfy the same needs as the previous rector, so some of the in-group will remain unhappy. The bonding process cannot be considered complete until the relations with these two groups have been worked out. Successful bonding requires that both groups perceive the new rector for the unique person that he or she is, and that they cease to perceive the new rector in terms of the previous rector.

Principle 8. *The healthy pastoral bond is centered in Christ.*

One of the grievous ills of priesthood is the temptation to the cult of personality. A parishioner says of us, "What a great priest!" and we believe it. We must be clear that we are not *The Priest*. We are the symbol of The Priest. This means that both we and our parishioners must find our center in Christ.

In behavioral terms this means that the center of parish life must be worship, and in worship you and I as persons must be transparent. We must be a symbol to the parish. Our persons must be subordinate to our office. Our vestments must signify more than our persons. We and the parishioners must focus on Christ.

Principle 9. *Listen to the heart of the parish.*

The heart of the parish is that group of parishioners who center in Christ by faithful worship, faithful giving, and faithful support and nurture of one another. They are the heart of the local Body of Christ and he is at their center. They are bonded to one another in him, and it is your bonding to them in him that is crucial. Listen to the heart. What do they tell you?

Principle 10. *The parish must be viewed not only from the perspective of the pastoral bond, but also from a long-term perspective, in terms of parish history and norms.*

You spoke of how parishioners were in conflict about your predecessor when you arrived, and you spoke of the harm you saw them doing to each other. What you were observing were the established norms of the parish for dealing with conflict, and if they were harmful, then you were observing patterns that need to be changed. Any decision you make about staying or leaving must take into account its effect on parish history and norms. Will your staying or your leaving help those norms be what they ought to be?

Principle 11. *You yourself have a history and a calling.*

You yourself are at a particular stage in your relation to God. He has brought you to where you are and he is calling you to take the next step, whatever that may be. Any decision about leaving or staying must take into account your own history and calling from God at this stage of your life. Let me now illustrate these principles in two controversies in my own experience.

I have been the focus of two parish conflicts in the past eight years. In one case I decided that I must leave. In the other I decided that I must stay.

Last year was my sixth at St. Richard's. At the end of our Annual Meeting a parishioner moved that the vestry be charged to evaluate the rector's performance and to report back to the parish with a list of changes to be made or with the rector's intention to resign. The motion was amended to include the possibility that the vestry might give the rector high marks, and then it passed. I asked for a vote of confidence and received it. As you might imagine, the meeting was very upsetting to me and to a lot of people.

I discovered later that the parishioner who made the motion had gathered a group ahead of time in support of it. I was not surprised by his hostility. Nor was I surprised that there were others who were hostile. Some had personal disappointments. Others were angry about some of my policies. My attempts at understanding and reconciliation had not borne fruit.

The vestry, which included both supporters (the majority) and critics, spent many hours doing the evaluation, basing it on the criteria of the Book of Common Prayer and the canons. It was very painful for them and for me. They were able to agree unanimously, however, on a written evaluation which said, in summary, that I was adequately fulfilling my duties, and they appended a list of specific perceptions, favorable and unfavorable, of my performance. I responded in writing, and then we circulated the documents in the parish. That took care of the charge given us by the Annual Meeting, but it did not end the controversy. Vestry meetings were painful. I dreaded them because at every meeting the critics harassed me about something. Two persons complained about me to the bishop. And during all of this I was filled with self-doubt. What had I done? How could I reconcile the complainers? And worst of all was the sinking feeling, the knowledge, that I couldn't do anything, that it was me they didn't like, me the way I am, and that it was my basic convictions that led to the disagreements in policy.

During this time I received lots of support. I felt confident of the large majority of the parish. But I was aware of critics who had stopped coming to church and of critics who had withdrawn financial support. It was clear that we were going to run a large deficit.

At vestry meetings I kept trying to respond to the critics. I kept insisting that we work on reconciliation and that we strive for consensus within the vestry. But finally it became evident that the dissenters would have none of it. They were going to oppose not only me . . . but anything I proposed.

This sort of strife was familiar in the parish. Some of the same people who were angry at me had circulated a petition seeking to get rid of my predecessor. Others had been angry at his predecessor. Power politics had been the parish norm.

I finally made two decisions. (1) I was going to stay. (2) I was going to work with those who were willing to work with me, and I was not going to allow the dissenters to bring us to a halt. From that moment everything got better. Our energies were no longer consumed by attempts to reconcile the irreconcilable. Vestry meetings became easier. We began to get things done. One of the dissenters resigned. Another rotated off. And at the Annual Meeting the dissenters failed to win any seats on the vestry.

During all of this our Sunday worship and our sense of fellowship went well. There was no sign that dissent was growing, quite the opposite. We gained a few new families, and—most striking of all—our pledge canvass resulted in a marked increase in giving.

The controversy at St. Peter's was different. It erupted in my fourteenth year as rector as a result of one action by me: I fired the music director. I can still see in my mind's eye the coffee hour after the news got out. People stood around in isolated groups, and when I entered the room I felt cut off. Our music program had been a source of immense parish pride, even though it had also been the source of immense problems.

In this case a lot of my friends were angry at me. We called a parish meeting and decided two things. We would hold a series of small group meetings between me and parishioners to see if things could be aired out and worked through, and we would get an outside consultant to help us find our way.

The small group meetings were excruciating for me. They be-

came garbage dumping grounds. Parishioners heaped on me complaints that were years old and that in many instances I had had no
awareness of. Vestry meetings were also painful. Friend was pitted
against friend. Vestry members who loved me and supported me
were now my critics.

Parish life went on pretty much as usual in terms of attendance
and giving and activities, but it hurt a lot. We were having a hard
time with each other.

The consultant talked with parish leaders individually and had a
session or two with the vestry. Finally he advised me that in his
judgment I had lost the confidence of the key parish leaders and
should leave.

This parish had been my parish for many years. I had chosen to
come to the neighborhood as a young man. I had been ordained
from the parish. My wife had been born in the neighborhood and
had grown up there. We had raised our children there. I felt a very
strong sense of identity with the parish. I had never considered
leaving. I wanted to stay, and I told the vestry so. We negotiated an
agreement. We would have a parish vote of confidence and allow
that vote to be our guide.

When the vote was taken I won by 60 percent to 40 percent.
That night I decided to leave.

These two controversies came to different conclusions and, I believe, the right ones.

First, the two controversies occurred at different stages in parish
life. Here at St. Richard's we were still engaged in the bonding process and were at the disillusionment stage. At St. Peter's we had
long before established the pastoral bond. Here we have been de-
ciding whether or not to go on to the stage of mutual acceptance.
There we were experiencing a trauma to the established bond. I
had struck a violent blow to that bond, and the question was
whether we could survive it.

Second, here there was a division between the heart of the parish and dissenters. There everybody (with but few exceptions) was
my supporter. Here it was the heart who wanted me to stay and
persons outside the heart who wanted me to go. There it was the
heart who said, "Bill, you've got to go."

Third, here the bonding process was proceeding successfully
with the heart. I became aware as the controversy went on that I
was in danger of abandoning the heart in order to appease a pow-
er-politicking group committed to other values and persons.

Fourth, here there was a history of divisions and of settling
them by a power struggle—in short, a history of unhealthy conflict.
There, there was no such history. The conflict was carried out with

a deep commitment by the leadership to the welfare of everybody involved. Here the dissenters sought to coerce others by withdrawal of support. There support continued throughout.

Fifth, there I felt overwhelmed. I remember those months as months of muteness. Whereas normally I am voluble, then I was subdued. Whereas normally I am filled with ups and downs of emotion, then I was overwhelmed with sadness. In contrast, my years here have been years of blossoming. I have done a lot of writing and new thinking, and have received a tremendous response. A flood of creativity has broken forth from me.

As I see it now, my firing of the music director was not only an attempt on my part to solve a deep parish problem, it was also, although I didn't realize it at the time, a blow for freedom, both for me and for the parish. As I see it now, I had become too identified with the parish and the parish with me. We were not two equal partners in a marriage. We were a merger of personalities. I was drowning and didn't know it. I needed to get free and didn't know it. And the parish needed to be free of me. They needed a rector with a strong sense of himself or herself as a person in his or her own right, a rector who would be more able to see them as they were and to confront them where they needed confronting.

Here at St. Richard's I am conscious of a different relation to the parish. I am conscious of a difference in me, of my ability to see them more objectively. Here I am much more conscious of the parish needs as distinct from my own.

The crucial difference in the two cases is signified by the tactics of the critics and their relation to me. At St. Peter's the critics were my friends, they cared about me and sought to see to my welfare, even while they criticized. At St. Richard's the critics were foes. They withdrew support of both me and the parish. They engaged in power plays. They valued the Lord's Table so little that they withdrew from it in an attempt at coercion. They had so little sense of bonding to the rest of the parish that they abandoned them too. St. Peter's had healthy norms of conflict. St. Richard's had unhealthy ones. My staying would not have helped St. Peter's; my leaving did us both good. My leaving St. Richard's would have done harm, for it would have reinforced the unhealthy norms of conflict. It would have strengthened the tactics of withdrawal and coercion, and it would have undercut the tactics of support and consensus-seeking.

There is much more to be said, of course. But perhaps the above will be of help.

> Your brother in Christ,
> Bill

NOTE

1. Readers from some traditions may find the term *The Priest* foreign. To catch the larger-than-life intent such readers should think of how Lutherans use the term *Pastor* and some Protestants use the term *Minister*. What is intended is the representational sense of the ordained ministry that evokes feelings and images of *The Person of God*, the one set apart to represent God's love and holiness for the People of God. *The Priest* may not be in his or her own person a holy man or woman, although some priests and ministers are; *The Priest* is the one who represents, *signifies* holiness. I suspect that this sign-aspect of ordained ministry is stronger in those traditions that emphasize the ordained minister's role as president of the sacraments, but I think it can hardly be absent from any tradition that ordains.

It is also important here to see that I am not making a theological claim. I am not saying that ordination causes such-and-such a change in the person. I am, instead, making an observation about what I observe actually happening. As a priest I find myself being experienced as *The Priest*, not just as a person. I find myself being experienced as larger-than-life. I also find myself sometimes being experienced as transparent; i.e., as not being experienced as a distinctive person at all.

For many years I fought against being seen in a larger-than-life way and against being unseen as a person. I resisted wearing clericals. I asked to be called by my first name. I defensively emphasized joint-ministry. But I found over and over again that many people still treated me differently from other persons, that many people *wanted* me to be different, that they wanted me to be something for them other than just myself. For that it was necessary that I become transparent, that Warner White disappear into the background and *The Priest* come into the foreground. I finally made a decision. I would do it. I would be *The Priest* for them. From then on wearing clericals was easy. It meant putting on my sign. It meant taking on the task of representing.

How Long Should a Pastor Stay?

by John A. Esau

How long should a pastor stay in a given congregation? Most of the time we avoid even asking that question for fear that we might be suggesting to our pastor that it's time to leave.

There is no right answer; indeed there are many answers to fit many different situations. But let me share some of my thoughts and observations.

I believe that we ought to begin with an assumption that our goal will be toward longer pastorates, meaning those in the range of eight to twelve years. There is an emerging consensus that the most significant years of ministry for a pastor begin after the fourth to sixth year. Does it really take that long to earn the necessary trust? Apparently so!

Some of our most competent pastors have made a personal commitment to themselves to serve in ten year cycles, giving them three to four different ministry experiences in a lifetime. Such pastors will choose to make a transition approximately every ten years, knowing that it is far better to move when all is positive and going well.

There are many factors today that need to be considered by pastors. Children, of course, must be taken into consideration. I fondly remember my own father turning down a significant opportunity so that I could complete my high school at Immanuel Academy (now High School) at Reedley, California.

Even more complex today is the part that a spouse plays in this decision. Wives of pastors have become professionals in their own right, and don't always willingly move. The even newer reality of husbands of pastors is making such decisions exceedingly complex for women in ministry.

Also to be taken into consideration is the place of the congregation in its development. Given our modern mobility (the average person moves every four years) there are some congregations in which the members are moving so often that the long-term pastor may be the only stable factor.

One pastor shared with me his struggle with this decision several years ago. He had led the congregation into a new era of change and growth. His ministry was at its peak and overwhelmingly positive, yet he chose to leave knowing how essential and yet how difficult it would be for him to lead the congregation into its next phase of growth. Recent contact with the congregation tells me that the new pastor is doing exactly what the previous pastor knew was needed, but which would have been nigh to impossible for him to do.

Over the life-cycle of a pastorate there is a gradual shift of the appropriate question which pastors should be asking themselves, from "Why would I leave?" to "Why should I stay?" In other words, in the early years the burden is to justify leaving, while as the years move on the burden shifts to justifying staying.

This is particularly true when one moves beyond the twelfth year in a given pastorate. One's own ministry may still remain positive, but what happens to the congregation when change finally comes? And what might that congregation experience with new leadership, recognizing the limitations that all of us have?

Then there is the issue of the pastor's own personal growth and development. Many persons who have made transitions when that decision was difficult bear witness to the revitalization that new places and new challenges in ministry bring.

Personally I am exceedingly grateful to be in a vocation in which occasional transition is expected. In terms of experiences, relationships, and personal growth which have come to me because of these transitions in ministry, I have been greatly enriched.

PART II

Leaving as an Occasion for Personal Growth

Often it is the transitions of life that are the greatest occasions for growth. In addition to appreciating what we are leaving and what we are moving to, we can learn many secrets of the Spirit by monitoring the experience of the transition itself. We can discover new things about ourselves and about the God who is with us in our transitions.

"Saying Goodbye: A Time of Personal Growth" by Craig Williams is the account of a young minister who, when confronted with a pastoral change, discovered that he never really "left home" successfully as a youth. Facing this transition became the occasion to become truly "individuated" and to face life and ministry as an adult.

"Living the Leaving" consists of excerpts from a two year period of the personal journal of Chandler Gilbert, from the time he first began to sense promptings to retire through the completion of the departure. It is a poignant description of his own feelings as well as those of parishioners.

A great temptation in leaving is not to own one's feelings of anger, loss, and grief. All who read "Tuck" Gilbert's testimony will be encouraged to take seriously the inward journey.

Saying Goodbye:
A Time of Personal Growth

by Craig Williams

Timing is everything—or so it is when telling a joke.

It is the same for leaving a pastoral position. But how to recognize that *kairos* moment which only God provides is difficult at best.

Last fall I left a position as associate pastor in which I had served for seven years, and several years as intern prior to that. I had worked for that same church from the time I was 18 until I was 34. The experience was rich and rewarding. When it came time to leave, however, I was confronted with a crisis I was ill-prepared to face.

Several times I was offered positions as the pastor of other churches, and each time there was something "wrong." Not usually with the churches themselves, but something was wrong with me. Everyone I sought advice from counseled me that I would know in my gut when it was the right call. The problem was, my gut-level feeling was always confused and uneasy. No situation seemed right for me, nor did I seem right for any of the positions. More than that, it was not a competency issue. I was more than competent for the positions I sought, but was unable to come to terms with any of them.

About my fifth year as associate pastor I felt the need to explore areas of ministry other than those then available to me. I was working as pastor to students and families in a church of 650 members. I had filled this position for ten years—five as associate pastor following my ordination, five before that as intern.

What piqued my curiosity was an invitation to submit my dossier to a new church development in northern California. This began a curious odyssey for the next two years, as I sought God's call to a ministry different from that in which I was involved.

This new situation caused me to take stock of myself and my

calling. There was a restlessness and a sense of turmoil inside as I struggled with where God wanted me to be, and what I wanted to be doing. Much of the turmoil I wrote off as my being tired of doing youth ministry for so many years, and the fact that I had a family and a different set of priorities. Some of it I wrote off as having been in one place for so many years.

As I finished my first year searching for a new call, what unfolded was something larger than any of the above issues. What began as a job search ended up becoming a soul-search. It was what is talked about in adolescent psychology as the process of individuation, and it has its roots far back in my childhood.

At this same time the church extended an invitation to me to change job descriptions and become pastor of congregational life. This was an intriguing possibility, one that I hoped would lead to new horizons and a new sense of call.

Instead, as the position approached I became increasingly depressed and unexcited. There was added pressure from the head of staff to become excited about this new calling. I had long prided myself on the fact that as an associate my first calling was to support the pastor of the church. This seemed to be coming to an end, as I was being asked either to enthusiastically embrace this new position, or move on as quickly as possible.

As I prayed and mulled over my decision I felt trapped. There was no quick way to move on in our denomination, and I felt that as long as I continued to remain on the fence concerning my call I could not wholeheartedly enter into the ministry at hand. With a great amount of reluctance I announced my intention to stay. At that moment I felt as though whatever light was at the end of my tunnel has just been extinguished. I was more depressed than ever before.

The pastor with whom I worked is a very intuitive man. I consider him to be much more than a colleague; he is one of my closest friends. My decision to stay had touched off a series of confrontations and disagreements unlike any we had known before. We had reached an impasse in our professional lives as well as in our friendship. As a result, we invited our local denominational representative to intervene. What ensued was a meeting between the three of us. We expressed our emotions. We debated philosophies and feelings. We explored staying and going. We argued and we listened. Then our colleague spoke to my friend and me. The first thing he said was that it was time for me to leave. To stay would be detrimental to all concerned. His next comment was that what I needed most was time. It could take two more years before a call might come to be the pastor of a church. It was the church's responsibility, he said, to give me the time to make a move. The third comment was the hardest: He said that what we were dealing with was a burned-out pastor.

My response was immediate. Two things flashed through my mind simultaneously: "No! Not me! I'm not one of those!"—pure denial. The second thought was, "Phew! It's out. I don't have to hide it any more!"—pure relief. But what it meant, and its relationship to my leaving, was still unsettled. The odyssey was to continue for some time to come.

Over the next twelve months I took the new position as pastor of congregational life. My short-term goals were focused on my new position and my long-term goals were focused on preparing to leave. There was light again at the end of the tunnel. The goals related to the new position were taking care of themselves. The long-term goals were a bit more muddled: How to make the move.

In that 12-month period I entered into a therapeutic relationship with a clinical social worker. Through this counseling relationship what unfolded was a past that impeded my ability to make a move in the present. A short history is in order.

My father was an alcoholic, my mother the enabler, and my sisters and I were the victims. This is a scenario that is too often repeated in the lives of our parishioners, and too often in those of us who are clergy.

I had read numerous books on adult children of alcoholics. There had been many conversations with people who had been in similar circumstances. There was a lot of understanding related to how it might affect someone's life. But up until this point the emotional impact had been fairly well hidden from me. Now I was in a place where the issues of the past had paralyzed me in the present—and were threatening to undo my future.

For most children a healthy adolescence means that they successfully leave home somewhere between eighteen and twenty-one. The key is *successfully*. A successful leaving means walking away and being able to turn and face your family, knowing your independence as well as your interdependence. To be able to say "I am on my own; I am my own person," and to have the approval of your parents as you stand apart from them, is a major developmental transition in our lives.

I left home at age eighteen and returned only briefly one summer when things began to get very tense between my parents. But my leaving was not successful. Rather, it was more of a running away—a survival technique.

All people who grow up in dysfunctional settings tend to be survivors. It enables them to get through the craziness. It also creates its own problems. I was a survivor. As my therapy unfolded more things about my past there was one incident that became something of a paradigm for my situation.

It was an incident that repeated itself over and over in my family. As my oldest sister entered college, the friction in our family increased. It seemed that the only time we were all together was at dinner, and as a result dinner was a most unpleasant experience. The meal was usually never finished as the arguments between my sister and my dad frequently squelched our appetites. One of the things that happened was that my middle sister and I were not allowed to leave the table as the fight raged on. We sat there unable to finish, unable to leave, waiting for my father to conclude. Then we would escape to the refuge of our rooms. The paradigm was the image of a ten-year-old sitting at the table while a disapproving and angry father refused to let him leave.

Though not analogous to my leaving the church, the very same feeling of helplessness had raised itself in the present situation, and in some twisted way was keeping me from being able to move beyond the present situation. There had been no successful leavings in my history, and there seemed to be no successful leavings in my future. There was no individuation in the past, nothing to draw on for the present. I was paralyzed, unable to go forward, because of the unfinished business of my childhood.

There had been many transfers of feelings from my past to my present. The church and my colleague had become my mother and my father. My feelings of having to sit at the table while the battle went on became the sinking feeling of being stuck in a job that I did not want. The extinguishing of the light at the end of the tunnel was the same as it had always been.

As each of these feelings was finally confronted, as the past became untangled from the present, things began to change. It was time to leave. It was time to successfully individuate for the first time in my life. Not to flee from a sinking ship, but to move confidently to a new call, to let the ghosts of the past die and allow the Spirit of God to begin a new work in me and my family.

On the seventh anniversary of my ordination I began a call as the pastor of a new church development in a community that is only three years old. At thirty-four years I had successfully individuated from my family—the church. Many of the past demons still raise their heads in hopes of distracting me and getting me off course. But they are at least manageable and able to be named.

My leaving was still emotional and difficult as I walked the last part of my odyssey. The goodbyes were tearful, and sometimes even bitter. There were unresolved issues and hurt feelings. There were many good memories and feelings of love. In the process I

believe I found my soul. It was the part that was missing as I unsuc-
cessfully tried to find the right call. It was the child sitting at the table without permission to leave. That child finally grew up.

When is it time to leave? When you are finished at the table of
one family and compelled to sit at the table of another, it is time.
When the ghosts of the past no longer impede your present, your
future, it is time. It is time to leave, not when things are simply difficult—that is running away, survival. It is time to leave when in the
fullness of God's time you can confidently give yourself fully to another part of Christ's body.

On Living the Leaving

by Chandler W. Gilbert

There are many possible reasons for leaving a parish. Perhaps
something has gone sour. Or, there seems to be nothing more one
can contribute. Or, the vision has disappeared and the "juice" is
gone, and discouragement, burnout, or loss of hope has taken over.
Or, a new opportunity has presented itself, and it beckons so excit-
ingly it cannot be resisted. Or, perhaps, a sense of calling from God
has been felt, which stirs the soul and simply must be followed,
even if it means leaving good friends and good work behind. Or,
all of the above.

The decision to leave is seldom the result of a sudden impulse.
In most cases, the seeds were planted long before, though perhaps
unrecognized at the time. In retrospect, one can discern them—the
early signs of a readiness to love, to hear a new call, to move out,
like Abraham, into a new and unknown future. In William Bridge's
words:

> Much as we long for external signs ... we must settle for inner
> signals that alert us to the proximity of new beginnings.[1]

Though I did not recognize it at the time, my journal was full of
hints of these seeds beginning to surface, the "inner signals," and
the pilgrimage they led me on, often without my knowing it. My
hope is that what follows will be helpful to others in the early
stages of considering a move, to those already well into the process
and to some who, having already made their move, are still won-
dering how to make sense of what happened. I trust it will portray
such diverse aspects of the process as the subtle (and not-so-subtle)
leadings of the Spirit, the doubts, the anxieties and fears that creep
into even the most valid of calls, the frequent waverings of faith and
the experience of unexpected grace, the ups and downs, the pain

and confusion, and the promise of eventual healing on the other side of the transition.

No two leave-takings are alike. If mine is unique in some respects, it still contains some emotional, spiritual, and physical universals. My "data," if they can be called that, come mainly from my journal, interspersed with a number of quotes and personal comments, the whole approach being deliberately very subjective. As Elizabeth O'Conner puts it:

> While . . . something is gained in the more conceptual and abstract statement, something is lost when we do not tell each other the story of how it was for us.[2]

This is the story of how it was for me.

Early Signals

9-18
Today is my 60th birthday. I do not *look* 60. I do not *feel* 60. But clearly, I am getting older. The hard part of growing old is the need to confront that which has not been, and to accept graciously what one begins to know will never be. There is some "giving up" about this. Or, is it rather "letting go"? With that there can sometimes be a loss of hope. But *can* there be, perhaps, in surrender and letting go a new level of acceptance, peace and joy? Right now I'm not sure.

Some friends gave me a sweatshirt for my birthday. On the front, in big letters, it said: MINISTERS DO IT WITH GRACE. I hope so!

2-26
I dreamed last night about a "house of horrors" where the doors came down and blocked my way, forcing me into a direction not planned. Other doors opened unexpectedly, offering me new choices. Everywhere there were snakes and spiders, all of them fake. But even though I knew they were fake, I was afraid they could panic me.

> A person on the top of a ladder is afraid of his footing. He may, somehow, some day, lose his standing, be sent hurtling down—again be a member of the ordinary citizenry.[3]

* * *

Looking back, I can see how tired I was. The tiredness, in fact, *became* one of the signals. I resonated strongly with the clergy person who was quoted as saying:

> I am appalled at what is required of me. I am supposed to move from sick-bed to administrative meeting, to planning, to supervising, to counseling, to praying, to trouble-shooting, to budgeting, to audio systems, to meditation, to worship preparation, to newsletter, to staff problems, to mission projects, to conflict management, to community leadership, to study, to funerals, to weddings, to preaching. I am supposed to be 'in charge,' but not *too* in charge, administrative executive, sensitive pastor, skillful counselor, public speaker, spiritual guide, politically savvy, intellectually sophisticated. And I am expected to be superior, or at least first-rate, in all of them. I am not supposed to be depressed, discouraged, cynical, angry, hurt. I am supposed to be up-beat, positive, strong, willing, available. Right now I am not filling any of those expectations very well. And I am tired.[4]

I *was* tired. I had been tired many times before. But this time it wouldn't go away. Days off, retreats, even vacations, did not provide the healing I felt I needed. My tiredness concerned me. I was not sure I could keep up this kind of life for another year or two, let alone five.

* * *

3/6

I am in a nose dive emotionally. Life feels totally out of control. Last night I could feel myself going down. I was not sure I could stop. I had visions of falling apart. My symptoms:

—Fed up with work. Approaching it as a heavy burden.
—Withdrawal at home, in social settings, in staff, in life. I'm not here. Don't bother me. Don't ask me to put energy into anything.
—Discouraged, depressed. What's the use?
—Anger—at Bobbie (my wife), at staff, at church, in traffic.
—Tears just below the surface.

I heard Robert MacFarlane on TV after his suicide attempt. He thought to himself, "The world would be a better place without me." No, I thought to myself, that's not how it feels. The way it feels to me is, "I would be in a better place without the world."

I think about quitting. But I have no idea what else I could do or would want to do.

I feel crowded, cluttered, boxed in.

I don't know what to do about it.

Simplify. Simplify. But how?

To come alive again, to pass through three dark zones: chaos, death, and pain.[5]

The transition stage ... is often signaled by growing feelings of discontent. The work we have been doing ceases to absorb us in the same way. Finally it seems impossible to endure until the weekend, or vacation, or retirement. The period is one of anxiety, sometimes experienced as boredom. One reaches toward the new without knowing what the new is. The transition stage is a difficult period because the old has lost its meaning, the new has not yet loomed into sight and one has doubts that it will come at all ... Only when looking back do we see into the new. Pain has kept us open in our waiting—asking, listening, looking, willing to make that journey into self—a journey few of us undertake with any seriousness until compelled by our suffering.[6]

3/7

Spiritually I have felt dry for a long time. In desperation I have returned to the lectionary and other nourishing things. The Benedictine method of prayer and Bible study works for me again! Scripture is potent.

Quiet time is my spiritual CPR—
breathing in/breathing out
love in/garbage out
light in/darkness out.

I have been reading Bob Raines' *A Faithing Oak.* Words and phrases grab me:

—"I am a dried up tree." (Isaiah 56:3)
—"The grace of re-foliation, restoration, re-birthing."
—"Pull me out of the net ... Be a sheltering rock to me." (From Psalm 31, JEB)
—"The Messiah comes to give us *space.*"
—"Deep is calling to deep." (Psalm 42:7)
—"He will bring everything together, everything." (Ephesians 1:9-10, JEB)

—"Let pass, dear brother, every pain; what lacketh you I'll bring
again." (quoted from Bonhoffer)
—"*Birthing* of hope; *healing* of memories."[7]

And so, in the midst of feeling like a dried-up tree, a seed of hope
is planted again, and I respond in my depths and am less scared
than I was, and not quite so dry.

3/17
I'm very aware of my need for space, and how I have failed to plan
for this on a daily basis.

Many of us are willing to be constantly available so as to be able
to keep on hugging the myth of our own indispensability.[8]

3/26
I'm feeling better. Some good time off. A relatively relaxed few days
at work. But last night a tough pastoral situation arose. I need to
deal with it today, and today was already too full. It deflated my energy. I woke up early feeling tired, tense, anxious, unable to go
back to sleep. I'm running too close to Empty. I can be very close
to Empty and still function perfectly well. But the very next moment
I'm out of gas and going nowhere. God said to Elijah, "Arise and
eat, or the journey will be too long for you" (1 Kings 19:7). I arise
each morning, and I eat. But there's not much in me, and it gets
used up fast.

I'm on a roller coaster of moods. I'm down, I'm up, I'm down,
sometimes swiftly and gut-wrenchingly.

5/26
My *attitude* toward the pace of my life is as counterproductive as
the pace itself. That is what I need to change. But the pace is destructive, too. That is clear, and I do not seem capable of changing it.

6/16
I find myself more and more uneasy about my place here in Concord.
I am very comfortable in some ways. But I am restless. I think the juices
really are drying up. It feels like time for a change, if not outward, then
inward—or both. I have no dreams. Nothing compels me or energizes
me. I am forgetful and neglectful. I am not doing my job well (though
I do not think most others are aware of that yet). I am not clear how
much of this is seasonal. If I am not doing better by fall I will know
this is trouble. There are stress and burn-out signals in all this. I
resonate with Bob Raines' words:

I am treading water, neither swimming nor sinking ... as
though there were bunches of insulation around my soul. Everything is muffled, hidden, under wraps, stifled. My dreams are
hidden from me now and my poetry is dried up. ... My entre-
preneurial engines are spinning the wheels where there is no
soil, no ... traction, just whining and whirring. ...[9]

"The Lord set me down in a valley of dry bones," said Ezekiel.[10]
I know about that valley. Annie Dillard calls us "frayed and nibbled
survivors" in a world stalked by chaos.

6/25

I discover the family is worried about me, and about what the pressures are doing to Bobbie and me. I am increasingly aware I am
not doing my job well, and in some ways I don't care. My motivation is extremely low. I am clearly in a mood to move on. But I
need a clearer picture of what I want to move *toward. Will it be
sufficient simply to change the externals?* Or is this more an *internal* problem?

Doors Begin to Open

When we are ready to make a beginning, we will shortly find an
opportunity.[11]

* * *

During this period two things happened that dramatically changed
the picture. Thanks to some inheritance, and some careful estimates
of the pros and cons of taking pension and social security earlier
than previously assumed, we began to see that finances alone were
not a compelling reason to stay in Concord. We *could* leave if we
chose to.

Second, some long-standing dreams of other forms of ministry
began to surface as something we could do now rather than waiting
until retirement. In short, as William Bridges said, "When we are
ready to make a beginning, we will shortly find an opportunity."[12]
Now that it seemed *possible* to leave, the question of whether we
really *wanted* to leave had an altogether different feel. Fears now
surfaced, not about staying, but about leaving. Resistance to the unknown, along with rekindled love for what I was doing and the
people I was working with created confusion and reassessment.

* * *

8/4

I am fearful of change. I feel some guilt at the thought of leaving the parish at 62 instead of 65. Early retirement seems to have some moral question marks attached. It seems too young. Will I find myself no happier, or perhaps even less so? Can I face the silent disapproval (or envy) of those who think it's a cop-out? So I debate within, and find few answers, other than a growing clarity that I do not feel any excitement at the thought of staying here much longer.

8/5

I am obsessed with the idea of leaving. Something has gone out of me where Concord is concerned. What frightens me is that something may have gone out of me, period, and I am not sure leaving will cure it. I have always said that when the juice is gone it will be time to leave. The juice is gone. I'd feel better if I knew what *does* have juice.

8/16

If I do not take care of the "deadness" in me it won't matter much whether I leave or stay. That's the bottom line. Step one is getting my inner fires stirring again.

8/19

I'm beginning to feel excitement. I really am ready to leave Concord. Or, at least, it is clear I am not wanting three or four more years here. So—it's time to go.

Meanwhile I will try to do "the plain duties of each day faithfully." I am not ready for a whole lot more.

The *freedom* to choose to leave has released me to see clearly how deeply I *desire* to leave.

9/7

I spent time alone today to listen to Bernstein's *Mass*. It was the high spiritual moment of the year for me. I laughed and I cried. The tears and the laughter both caught me by surprise. I haven't *felt* so deeply in a very long time.

The part that stirred me most was near the end, where the Celebrant shatters the Communion setting. The accompanying description tells how he strips off his vestments, and says to the people with fervor and anger, "What is it you are waiting for? Just go on without me. Stop waiting. What is it about me you've been respecting? And what have you been expecting? Take a look. There is nothing but me under this ... What, are you still waiting? Still waiting for me, alone, to sing you into heaven? Well, you're on your own.

..." And then the boy soprano begins the "Lauda," a simple song. And then a bass picks it up, and they sing together. Then two chains of embraces begin, and the simple song builds. The Celebrant enters unobtrusively from the side, dressed simply now, without vestments, and all whisper "Peace be with you." The boy's choir goes into the aisles and brings the touch of peace, and says, with each touch, "Pass it on."

Why does that move me so deeply?

I feel the burden of the vestments and the office, the strange respect I am given, the awesome, unreal expectations placed upon me. And I sense my aloneness in that I seem to be expected to sing them/pray them/preach them/pastor them into heaven—me alone. And I want to strip the vestments, and all the rest, and say to them, "What have you been expecting? Take a look, there is nothing but me under this"—and let the song begin to come from them in new ways.

The Pain of Coming Alive

The pain of coming alive is mixed with pleasure. It is always a surprise when it begins to happen.[13]

9/17 (One year since my 60th birthday)
Yesterday I was unbearably eager to move on. I am thinking about things I want to *do*. I am distracted from the tasks at hand. *I am feeling freed!*

10/1
Things are happening awfully fast. We have found our house. It has all the features we had listed. Mostly I am excited. But there is anxiety, too. And always questions, questions.Today the house and the newcareer seem very unreal. Other days, it is so real I can taste it.

One step at a time. . . .

10/20
The anxieties about the unknowns multiply. The impact of our decision feels enormous.

10/22
I look for some guidance from God. It occurs to me that the guidance has already been given.

11/5

Fenhagen's question, "Is it well with your soul?" haunts me. I do
not think it is well with my soul. God is more like an absentee
landlord just now. The *unknowability* of God is dominant at the
moment. I say that, oddly, just when I am feeling God's leading
quite clearly.

I review my ministry. I see my successes, and they feel good.
But I feel some sense of failure, too. So *much* activity and hard
work, so little change in heart, belief, life-style, understanding, commitment, prayerfulness. Concord's pace is unhealthy for the soul. It
contradicts the life of the Spirit. It is dangerous to one's health. It is
dangerous to one's soul. It is dangerous to one's marriage. It is not
"the good life" it is cracked up to be. Is this just Concord? Of
course not. But it does *include* Concord. There is danger in the
suburbs, not just in the city. I have *no idea* what to do about it. I
may even have contributed to the disease.

My own mood shifts daily. Today I'm down-ish again. I have had
a couple of very scary dreams that seem to me to be saying, "What's
going on in your life just now is a whole lot scarier than you have
let yourself realize. So why don't you just take your scaredness
more seriously and stop ignoring, pretending, burying, repressing
it?" My unconscious is my friend, and needs to be listened to.

Separation Begins in Earnest

11/29

I feel myself already separating from the church. I am less invested,
more distanced, less compulsive.

The options available to me in my prospective new setting are
far more exciting to me than the ones where I am now. I know, of
course, that I will take with me all my propensity for busy-ness and
fracturedness and anxiety, and my tendency to feel guilty if I am not
working hard, and all the other quirks that will not go away when I
move. "Hell is portable," I am told. So am I.

I am beginning to feel anxious about the anger and misunderstanding we are likely to experience from various people once our
decision is made public.

12/22

I am struggling with my preaching. It feels flat. I am groping
around in old sermons to find repreachables.

12/23

It is uncanny how relaxed I have become. I am clearly "separating."
The move is constantly on my mind, almost always pleasurably. But
the more relaxed I become, the harder it is to remember why I am
leaving!

I have very few doubts about the decision. It seems right. But
every so often I have to work it through again in my head.

This morning I said to God, "What *is* your will, *really*?" And the
answer that came to my mind instantly was, "I already told you."

* * *

How *does* one know the will of God? My father used to like to tell
me the eight steps suggested by a great Christian by the name of
Henry Drummond. They went something like this:

1. Pray.
2. Think.
3. Talk to wise people, but do not regard their opinions as final.
4. Beware of the bias of your own will, but do not be too much
   afraid of it either.
5. In the meantime, do the next best thing, for doing God's will
   in small things is the best preparation for doing it in great
   things.
6. When decision and action are necessary, go ahead.
7. Never reconsider the decision, once it has been acted upon.
8. You will probably not find out until afterward, perhaps long
   after, that you have been led at all.

* * *

Getting Ready to Announce the Decision

12/24

The approaching date for announcing my resignation makes me
nervous. Partly this is awareness of the shock and pain it will create.
Partly it is knowing that this will be the point of no return. The die
will be cast. No turning back.

1/13

My stomach does flip-flops at the thought of breaking the news next
week. This is going to be *hard*.

Last night at the Diaconate meeting I listened and looked and loved them all. Good, good people! I will miss them. I recoil from hurting them or disappointing them.

1/17
I am feeling very insecure. I am deliberately, of my own free choice, turning my back on some of the people and tasks I love most in this world. I am leaving behind people who have loved me and affirmed me beyond belief. I need to accept that this is scary. And I need to keep returning to the dream of what lies ahead.

1/18
Today we had our Moderator and Assistant Moderator come to our house for breakfast, and we told them our decision. They were affirming and excited for us. I wonder what feelings they did not express.

I had a pain in my gut. It persisted most of the day.

Soon, perhaps, I will allow myself the beginnings of grief. So far (except for the pain in my gut) I am not feeling much.

"Play it cool, and you will soon be frigid."[14]

Reactions: Anger, Disbelief, Ambivalence, Distancing, Support, Love, and Grief

* * *

One of the most helpful things about Roy Oswald's writing about termination of a pastorate was his vivid reminder of the kinds of emotions a resignation can set loose. Without that warning, I would have been shaken badly by some of the things that happened after our decision became public. Even so, it was startling to me. Again, my journal suggests at least some of what is set loose.

1/20
Today we told our church secretary, a very special lady. We knew this would be hard for her. She was visibly shaken.

Later in the day I told our Advisory Group. One man made an immediate response—really quite beautiful, thoughtful, affirming. He spoke of the importance of following a dream, and I was touched by his words. As the meeting proceeded, however, he became extremely pessimistic, predicted doom for the church. His face was contorted in a way I had never seen it. I did not know if it was anger, or grief, or both. He and another man, both good friends of mine, left after the meeting without a word or a handshake. The anger and hurt is already visible. I dread the coming weeks.

I am feeling some anger, too. So *much* of the responsibility for the well-being of this church gets laid on *me*.

1/21
Another very hard day of telling staff and phoning key people.

I realize there is one thing, at least, that I cannot share openly with people, and that is how eager I am to leave.

1/24
This was the Sunday to say it from the pulpit, following up the letter they all received yesterday.

I am truly astonished by the depth of people's feelings about me. There were some sweet, gentle, tender moments with B.T., a man I have talked with at length about some of his personal problems. Also with H.J., the tough guy, the macho man, who got all choked up. Two other men, also. I was told that after J.B. read the letter, he wept. I was surprised that it was men, not women, whose emotions came to the surface most quickly.

The angriest reactions are from those who need me most—or think they do. The ones who are most needy, most scared, most hurt are the ones who lash out.

I am touched by letters and phone calls from *outside* the parish. Friends outside the parish are almost unanimously enthusiastic about our plans.

People are often very awkward. Many do not know what to say, and so they avoid me. We have had only one or two calls from parishioners. I had expected the phone to ring off the hook. One woman, usually one of the warmest and most approachable, was distant and cold as ice when I met her on the street.

1/27
After Church Committee last night our Moderator burst into tears in my study. The burden on her is heavy. I feel really bad about what my leaving is creating for others, and especially for her. She feels betrayed. There is a panic reaction in some of the leaders. Their proposals for how to rescue the church from this "disaster" are not on target. Their intensity is almost frightening. Came home from the meeting feeling sad and a bit guilty.

The coming seven months look too long. I want to get going.

The silence continues. Very few phone calls. They just don't know what to say (or are afraid to say it).

2/3
Last night was our Annual Meeting. My last. I felt little emotion about that, unlike two Sundays ago, when I could just barely hold myself together.

The congregation was depressed. We had a hymn-sing, and no one seemed interested in choosing hymns, contrary to their usual eagerness.

I felt very proud of this church as its leaders spoke, and was re-assured of its continuity and strength.

I get slight twinges of feeling left out as they begin to take hold in new ways. I feel less important, less needed. Leaving has really begun.

2/11

Today, one of the worst staff meetings in history. Some of them wandered in late; some found reasons to come and go during the meeting. One yawned out loud! The agenda got subverted into nit-ty-gritty and miscellany. By the end of the meeting, one was obvi-ously near tears. One was visibly frustrated. Another is grieving and lost. Another is asking if I will still be her friend. They are disorga-nized, tense, and anxious.

2/14

Two key leaders buttonholed me after church today full of concern about the upcoming planning night, complaining about the time it is scheduled for, and predicting no one will come. They finally is-sued a kind of "threat"—"It better be *good*," they said. It felt to me like an ultimatum.

I feel really angry at the hints of threat and panic.

One man resigned from a key committee. I do not believe he would be doing this if I were not leaving.

I need to remember that grief takes *time*—mine and theirs. It had only been three weeks for them. I keep forgetting that to some this is like a death. To others it is abandonment.

I love being loved. But I resent being treated, at times, like they *own* me.

2/19

The man who resigned finally put it into words. He says he feels as if he is at my funeral whenever we talk about my leaving. He finds it too painful. I do not know how to help him. I need to find a way to get together with him and get it out in the open between us.

The Roller Coaster Continues

All of my past virtues have become vices. Hard work, com-mitment, and willpower do not serve me well in this time. I must face the soft feelings of grief and confusion. I must remain vulnerable to the trembling.[15]

2/20

Tensions grow between Bobbie and me—mostly old stuff raised to new levels. A wall grows between us. It is scary to feel this in the midst of so much other pain and confusion.

2/21

I feel strangely at peace today, more at ease. I turned to my "Twenty-four Hours a Day" booklet, given me by an AA friend, and read, "When I feel the calm of my spirit has been broken by emotional upset, then I must steal away alone with God until my heart sings and all is strong and calm again." Yes!

3/3

The wall with Bobbie is down. I am at ease in myself. A lot of my anger is dissipated. I am much less irritable.

The planning night went superbly well. But a Diaconate meeting went sour. I felt partly to blame for what happened. I have tremendous investment in seeing things go well these coming months.

3/4

The day plummeted. I felt inadequate, angry, anxious, near tears. Surprised at the depth of my emotions.

4/27

I have been on a plateau. No major ups or downs. Pressure on the job has been minimal. I am feeling somewhat separate from the people, and they are feeling somewhat separate from me. Usually the distancing feels good. But last night it hit me—I am feeling unwanted, unneeded, useless, superfluous—and a bit rejected!

It's lame duck time.

Thank God for old sermons. I can't seem to create new ones. This is *fallow* time.

5/15

I am increasingly aware of "last times"—the last Maundy Thursday service, the last Easter, the last Confirmation class, etc. When I take time simply to sit and reflect, the sadness surfaces. When I am very busy I scarcely feel it at all. I need to do more sitting and reflecting.

5/26

The tension grows. I find myself questioning my move. I am getting prickly and irritable at home, with Bobbie and with myself. The weeks are flying by, and each Sunday is lump-in-the-throat time. Goodbyes begin to feel real.

I am not sleeping well. I wake early with the spring sunlight and the birds, and cannot get back to sleep. I am more tired. No readiness for devotional life and good reading or journaling. I am hurried and distracted.

I feel like a "veteran of inner wars."

6/5

My sister, Mariel, told me today that I seemed distant, distracted, and sad. I agreed with distant and distracted, but disclaimed the sad. Then she left, and I spent the next hour wanting to cry. She had named the sadness, and by naming it helped release it. She was right. There is, increasingly, a sadness pervading my days. My emotions are closer to the surface. I can *feel* the leaving and am starting to dread it. I am not as eager as I was. I begin to sense the enormity of what we are about to do, and it frightens me. I view the church, the town, this house, and yard where I have lived for 17 years, and I feel new appreciation.

I am self-centered now. I do not put much effort into relationships. I make less effort to listen, to probe, to draw others out, to connect. I am into my own stuff, and not much interested in theirs.

My body is acting up also. I have a pain under my right rib cage. My doctor is checking it out—thoroughly. Tests, tests, more tests. I am losing weight. I begin to feel anxious about all the terrible things it could be, even though I really don't believe that is the case.

6/26

Last Sunday was the big farewell party. A beautiful morning worship service, with a farewell ritual included. Everything done just right. Then a wonderful, upbeat celebration under a huge tent. Music, laughter, skits, all done with flair and with love.

The pressure is off. But the pain in my chest is worse. Can't laugh, hug, or sleep comfortably. More tests. It nags at me and colors all my days. Moving and packing feel ominous in this condition. Is my body confronting me with the pain of leaving? Is it saying to me, "This is more painful than you seem to realize, and if you won't let yourself feel the pain in appropriate ways, I'll make you feel it this way"? Or, perhaps, since it hurts so much to laugh, is my body saying, "This is just to remind you that leaving is no laughing matter"?

6/30

Today I am fighting fear. More tests ordered by the doctor. I sense he is worried about me. I have cold waves of fear they will find something like cancer.

More Spiritual Ups and Downs

> Then comes a time of numbness. The body freezes to pro-
> tect us against further pain; the . . . armor tightens to guard us
> against the onslaught of the strange, new world. Our defenses
> keep us from feeling anything—terror or hope.[16]

7/12

I woke very early, and found myself in prayer. I imagined God saying to me, "Tuck, you started on this road—don't cop out now—
keep going." And I felt reassured. But it didn't last.

I have lost touch with God and my sense of calling, and am having a hard time of it. I still cannot believe we have the money to
make this change, no matter how I figure and refigure. There *is* a
risk. There *is* a cutting loose from all the security of a pay check
and a free parsonage. I have lost my courage. At times I am terri-
fied. I have little faith that God is really involved and will lead me
and provide for the journey. Abraham is a hero to me precisely because he did so wholeheartedly what I am about to do so fearfully.
But then, on second thought, maybe Abraham was anxious, too! But
he set out anyway. The thought comforts me. I have gotten discon-
nected from my Source. This is the heart of it. This is where I need
to begin—not with finances, but with the Source.

I am seeing that all new ventures have these components of self-
doubt, anxiety, and fear, whether it is Abraham setting off for a future he does not know, or a guy setting out to climb Mt. Everest or
sail around the world, or start new business, or whatever.

I wish for the ability to see my doubts, anxieties, and fears not
as aberrations or weakness or failure on my part, but simply as part
of the journey itself, just as demanding as rivers and mountain
ranges and injuries that have to be overcome. I wish to make this
move with full recognition of its difficulties (mostly inner ones), but
also with eagerness, excitement, and flair. If I make mistakes—or
even if the whole thing turns out to be a mistake—I'd like to accept
this as one of the braver and more exciting and imaginative mistakes of my life, made in good faith, with good counsel, with creative energy and intent, and a clear sense of it being what God
wants. So, full steam ahead! Give it my best shot!

7/16

Anxiety has me by the short hairs again. I can't seem to shake it. I
am even anxious about being anxious. I tell myself to "let go, let
God"—but I can't manage it.

No new time of life is possible without the death of the old life-time. To gain, you must first give up.[17]

7/31
This is my final Sunday. I am close to tears.

Renewal Begins—A New Way Opens

8/28
The move is done. Wonderful friends, hard-working crews from the church helped us paint, and brought carloads of our stuff. Concord feels a hundred years ago.

Today I made time for reading, and quiet, and writing. It felt wonderful; I need more of this.

These lines touched me especially:

> Listen to me
>   under my words
>   where the shivering is,
> in the fears
>   which freeze my living . . .
> in the doubts
>   which chill my hoping.[18]
> Gentle me . . .
>   into an unclenched
> moment,
>   a deep breath,
>   a letting go
>   of heavy expectations,
>   of shrivelling anxieties,
>   of dead uncertainties.[19]

So often I want to be "dead certain," forgetting that to be dead certain *is* to be dead, somehow. I felt some burden lift.

12/2
I *love* this place! It feeds my deepest needs. The woods, the lane, the stone walls, the mountain away in the background—all are very deeply pleasing to me, and peaceful. To steal a phrase from May Sarton, the world around me "rinses my eyes."[20]

I am rediscovering myself (painfully, at times), and life feels good. But there is something yet to be grasped. Not sure what it is.

12/13

I am disorganized, inefficient, frustrated by the length of my "To Do" lists. I know these feelings well! I came here, in part, to escape them. This is my accustomed mode.

My body has improved some, but it still hampers me and limits my strength and activity levels. I may just need to learn to accept my limitations gracefully and graciously. But I'm not quite ready to settle for that.

> All of us must accommodate ourselves to the simple fact that we are not so young as we once were, and thus take life in the stride belonging to the years we have lived. Help us make the noblest use of mind and body in our advancing years. . . . Teach us to bear our infirmities with cheerful patience.[21]

To all that, I say, "Yes, *but* . . .!" It seems to me a prayer, more to be prayed at 75 or 80 than at 62!

12/18

Emotions are running deeper these days. Or am I simply more open to them? It feels good to feel *good*!

12/30

The future is before me. I am aware I do not know how to do this new thing.

> The time has come
> To stop allowing the clutter
> To clutter my mind
> Like dirty snow,
> Shove it off and find
> Clear time, clear water
>
> ....
>
> To untie every knot,
> To take the time to dream,
> To come back to still water.[22]
> Eternal Friend,
> grant me an ease
> to breathe deeply of this moment,
>   this light,
>   this miracle of now . . .[23]
>
> O Lord,
>   in the turbulence
>   of my living . . .

keep me in touch with my roots . . .
keep me in touch with my feelings . . .
keep me in touch with my mind,
keep me in touch with my dreams . . .[24]

Pry me off dead center . . .[25]
Help me to believe in beginnings,
   to make a beginning,
     to be a beginning,
so that I may not just grow old,
   but grow new . . .[26]

Move with me now
   in my time of new beginnings . . .
I tremble on the edge of a maybe,
   a first time,
     a new thing,
     a tentative start,
and the wonder of it lays its finger on my lips . . .[27]

O patient God,
make something new in me
   in this year
     for you.[28]

Postscript

The journey continues. Adjustments are not over. Just as grieving the loss of a loved one is never completely done, so with transitions. Not all transitions will be as turbulent as mine has felt to me. Some, perhaps, will be even more so. But life is to be lived as fully as possible in each moment. We are not meant to miss the turbulence. We need not go through our experiences numb and only half alive, with "bunches of insulation" around our souls.[29]

If you would "live the leaving" fully, I commend the keeping of a journal from the first subtle signals on. When you feel yourself trembling on the edge of a maybe, let yourself be vulnerable to the trembling. Be aware of the seedlings seeking to surface in you. Watch them grow. Seek to know what God is telling you in them. Recall the books and devotional materials you have found most fertile in the past, and find them again, and keep them at your fingertips. You'll need them. Over and over, seek to discover God's will, following the wisdom of Henry Drummond listed earlier. Pray.

Think. Talk to wise people. And you may not know until later, much later perhaps, that you have been led at all.

May God bless your going out and your coming in. And may your journey be rich and good!

NOTES

1. William Bridges, *Transitions: Making Sense of Life's Changes* (Reading, MA: Addison-Wesley Publishing Co., 1980), 136.

2. Elizabeth O'Conner, *Cry Pain, Cry Hope: Thresholds of Purpose* (Waco, TX: Word Books, 1987), 13.

3. Robert Coles, *The Moral Life of Children* (Boston: Atlantic Monthly Press, 1986), 206.

4. Barbara G. Gilbert, *Who Ministers to Ministers? A Study of Support Systems for Spouses* (Washington, DC: The Alban Institute, 1987), 3.

5. Sam Keen, *Beginnings Without End* (New York: Harper & Row, 1975), 6.

6. O'Conner, op. cit., 14–15.

7. Robert Raines, *A Faithing Oak: Meditations from the Mountain?* (New York: Crossroads, 1982), 55–56.

8. Ibid., 35.

9. Ibid., 55–56.

10. Ezekiel 37:1.

11. Bridges, op. cit, 136.

12. Ibid.

13. Keen, op. cit., 6.

14. Ibid., 10.

15. Ibid., 5.

16. Ibid., 6.

17. Bridges, op. cit., 152.

18. Ted Loder, *Guerrillas of Grace* (San Diego, CA: LuraMedia, 1984), 16.

19. Ibid., 17.

20. May Sarton, *The Silence Now: New and Uncollected Earlier Poems* (New York: W. W. Norton & Co., 1988), 20.

21. Howard Thurman, *Deep is the Hunger: Meditations for Apostles of Sensitiveness* (New York: Harper & Bros., 1985), 124–125.

22. Sarton, op. cit., 15.

23. Loder, op. cit., 22.

24. Ibid., 90.

25. Ibid, 97.

26. Ibid, 99.

27. Ibid, 110.

28. Ibid, 116.

29. Raines, op. cit., 55.

PART III

On Knowing How to Say Goodbye

Saying goodbye is not just a matter of mastering certain techniques. Often separation calls into question our sense of self and our trust in God. It tests our ability to let go of the past and to risk the uncertainty of the future. Scott Peck, a well known psychologist, has written about this process of growth:

> True adults are those of us who have learned to continually develop and exercise their capacity for transformation. Because of this exercise, progress along the journey of growth often becomes faster and faster the further we proceed on it. For the more we grow, the greater becomes our capacity to be empty—to empty ourselves of the old so that the new may enter and we may thereby be transformed[1]

This anthology offers two articles on the basic art of saying goodbye well. In "Reflections On Ending Ministry in a Congregation," Ingram Parmley describes some of the dysfunctional behaviors that otherwise successful pastors may engage in after announcing their resignation. He points out that termination is not accomplished by an announcement, but is rather a process, "an ongoing sequence of events, feelings, actions, and interactions."

In the article "The Pastor Says Goodbye" Anthony Plathe talks about saying goodbye using the categories developed by Elisabeth Kubler-Ross in her book *On Death and Dying*.[2] A congregation and pastor can go through the stages of denial, anger, bargaining, resignation, and acceptance just as a person facing death.

NOTES

1. M. Scott Peck, *The Different Drum* (New York: Simon & Schuster, 1987), 181.
2. Elisabeth Kubler-Ross, *On Death and Dying* (New York: Macmillan, 1969).

Reflections on Ending Ministry in a Congregation

by Ingram C. Parmley

The typical parish minister never has an opportunity to see a congregation in its life and work between the departure of the previous pastor and the arrival of the new one. He or she either creates the hiatus by resigning, or ends it by arriving to take up a new ministry in the congregation.

Sometimes the outgoing minister adds to the problems of the congregation.

Because they see the congregation from within, parish clergy do not always see the negative consequences of their leave-taking, including the last minute events and situations that they help create on their way out the door. No one can be expected to be fully objective about such leave-takings. But they can be aware of the process and attempt to minimize the possibility of damage.

This damage can take many forms. One minister, leaving a rather troubled situation, suddenly "felt led" to withdraw his resignation. The result was more confusion, hurt, and anger added to that already experienced by the congregation.

Another pastor remained in the office of his former parish a week after his furniture had been moved and two weeks after the termination of his tenure with the parish, "helping out" the former parish with its plans for a Lenten program. His extended time in the former parish was made possible because his new congregation had graciously provided for him to take a vacation before assuming his new duties!

Yet another pastor spent the last few days in his old parish dreaming up and scheduling an Advent program requiring several visiting speakers with attendant travel expenses and honoraria of which the governing board knew nothing and for which no funds were budgeted.

Then there are many examples of the pastor who publicly proclaims his or her relief and joy at being able to leave the current parish without indicating any of the ambivalence and sadness attendant upon leaving old, good, and familiar friends and places.

And these are ministers who have been happy and productive in the parishes from which they were moving!

Leaving a parish is difficult if for no other reason than having to pack all that *stuff* and move it. But there is perhaps more potential for trouble in the situation which has been happy, than in one which has been unhappy.

Social psychologists would explain the ambivalent behavior described above as resulting from an "approach-approach" conflict. That is, the conflict lies in the attraction of the familiar parish and all it offers and the attraction of the new position and its potential. Each presents an "approach" condition: we wish to *approach* desirable situations, rather than to avoid them.[1] It is like wanting to have your cake and eat it, too. Both conditions are attractive.

I believe many clergy in preparing to move develop destructive or negative behavior to resolve the psychic conflict within themselves. This comes about, not out of demonic, unconscious forces, but because most do not take time to reflect on what the change in jobs is likely to mean, and what they are likely to experience and feel during the transition period.

This phenomenon was first brought to my attention many years ago when a rehabilitation counselor told about the different positions he had held with his agency. Each time he was transferred he had accidentally broken a stopwatch while testing a client on the last day he worked in the position he was leaving. He had been quite happy in each of the four positions!

Is it possible that we behave in negative ways to reduce the positive feeling we have for people and places we are leaving behind?

Terminating a relationship is not accomplished by an announcement. It is a process, an ongoing sequence of events, feelings, actions, and interactions. Making the decision to leave and announcing it to a congregation is the beginning of the process, not the end of it. The process will continue for the minister into his or her tenure in the new parish.

For instance, requests to return to the former parish for various occasions and functions such as weddings and funerals may continue for years after one's leaving.

The process need not be destructive. In addition to becoming aware of it, the minister can do certain things that can help make it a more positive experience for all involved.

How does the pastor minimize the damage to the congregation he or she is leaving, damage resulting from the pastor's own failure to recognize and/or cope with the multiple emotions and motives stirred up in the process of leaving? My experience tells me that there are several things the departing pastor can do to ease the transition both personally and for the congregation being left behind. If you are about to create a vacancy (or expect to sometime in the future) the following suggestions may merit your consideration:

1. *Activate your spiritual awareness.* If ever you need to operate out of a rich personal spiritual life, this is the time. It can also be a good time for a private retreat, to marshall your inner resources and listen for the guidance of the Holy Spirit. An ongoing prayer/support group is a resource of tremendous help. Knowing others are praying with you and for you as you make this transition can be comforting and encouraging. This is a good time to study again the Pastoral Epistles searching for guidance in ministry; and Paul's letters and their teaching about the mission of the church. A good spiritual director can be very helpful.

2. *Leave quickly.* The fear of leaving too quickly is largely unfounded. A month seems to be adequate notice of your intentions to leave your present position. Sixty days is more than adequate. Even clergy who are preparing to retire can help by postponing *formal* announcement until the last two or three months before their departure date, though "everyone" already knows. The longer the time between announcement of an impending departure and the actual time of leaving, the greater the temptation to exercise inappropriate influence and control over the life of the congregation. Remember, once you have announced your leaving, your role in that congregation will be changed. You become a temporary resident, someone who is passing through, where previously your presence and ministry were seen as permanent, dependable, to be counted on.

3. *Monitor your moods.* Keep an ongoing written account of your moods and important events. It should be written for your private use, so that you can be fully honest about the process as it unfolds. Refer to it frequently. You will be likely to see recurring patterns of action, and to connect them to your moods and perceptions. Writing is also a good way to plan. There is something about putting things down in writing that gives organization to our thoughts and feelings. Writing is a way of carrying on a conversation with yourself. It is one form of discipline you can use in assessing your own intentions and behaviors.

4. *Share pertinent information and feelings.* Let the congregation in on what is happening. This can be done through letters, newsletters, and church suppers, as well as in informal conversation. Being open about your ambivalent feelings is not only good

for you and helpful for your leaving; it can also serve as a model
for parishioners. Your behavior can help others to feel that it is
good and proper for them to express their own feelings openly and
freely.

5. *Maintain appropriate communications channels.* This means
you must keep church officials informed in some detail. They can
be sources of feedback from the congregation. Your advice from
this time forward is not likely to be helpful if it is not restricted to
the day-to-day operation of the parish. Likewise, the details of leaving are likely to be accomplished more smoothly if your governing
board is not having to hear every detail of your call to the new parish or your expectations of life in that new place.

Needless to say, the less you have to say about your successor
the better off everyone will be. Mentioning names of likely candidates can be particularly disastrous.

6. *Contract for exit consultation.* Ask a skilled pastoral counselor
to act as a monitor for you, to help you ask the right questions and
face the difficult issues as you prepare to exit the scene. This
consultant should be a friend, and reasonably objective. Be careful not
to choose someone for this role who will simply give you uncritical
support. If you have to pay a consultant fee for this service it will be
money well spent. A consultant who is a fellow pastor will probably
be more objective if he/she does not live in the same community with
you. A fellow staff member is likely to be less than helpful unless he or
she is exceptionally skillful and mature.

Note that the exit consultant role is different from that of the
spiritual director mentioned above.

7. *Express appreciation for valuable gifts received.* A final word
to your congregation in which you acknowledge your actions and
feelings not only will help you maintain your integrity and reputation, but can be healing for the congregation which must now
grieve its loss of you. Gratitude expressed to them for their ministry
to you as well as for the opportunity to minister to them should be
a part of this confessional and intimate moment.

What all of this is attempting to say is that while there is usually
some tension and anxiety present in pastors and parishioners at
moving time, the thoughtful pastor can turn that into creative tension by becoming aware of her own ambivalence, monitoring his
own behavior with the help of others, and letting church officials
and parishioners in on what is happening.

Sharing the tensions provides an opportunity for growth for all
involved and reduces the sense of isolation that all can feel at such
a time.

Many things will be occuring during moving time: calls and letters from the new parish, packing to move, saying goodbyes, leaving the office in good shape. But the church and its Lord will be well served by careful planning for the pastor's last days in town.

NOTE

1. Kurt Lewin was a pioneer in explaining internal conflicts. In *A Dynamic Theory of Personality* (New York: McGraw-Hill, 1935), he explored this form of conflict as well as what he called "approach-avoidance" conflict and "avoidance-avoidance" conflict.

The Pastor Says Goodbye:
How to Move through Good Friday to Easter

by Anthony H. Plathe

Leaving a parish after serving as pastor for a number of years is a difficult and often painful experience for the pastoral minister as well as the parish community. Yet I have come to believe that we can find new meaning in the process of change and transition by relating it to the dying and rising of Christ.

One of the apparent contradictions found in Christianity is that we must die to have new life. Our souls grow by subtraction. To the extent that we are able to let go of fear, power, control, and possessions, we are free people. In John 12:24 Jesus said, "I solemnly assure you, unless the grain of wheat falls to the earth and dies, it remains just a grain of wheat. But if it dies, it produces much fruit." In verse 26, he continues, "If anyone would serve me, let him follow me; where I am, there will my servant be."

During every pastoral transition,[1] some dying occurs in the one who leaves and in the church community left behind. I believe the feelings experienced are similar to the stages of physiological dying that Elisabeth Kubler-Ross presents in her important book, *On Death and Dying*.[2] As we move through these stages, it's helpful to remember that Jesus, through His own dying and rising, has preceded us in this process. Because we are human and do not easily embrace pain, we need the Lord's help as we go through the process of dying and letting go.

"Say it isn't so."

Many people facing a difficult transition experience denial—refusing to face reality because it's too painful and unpleasant. How each of us manifests denial varies. In *Running Through the Thistles*[3], Roy M. Oswald illustrates one approach.

As a young boy, Roy and his two older brothers often took a shortcut to school through an enormous thistle patch. In some places the prickly patches were 50 to 100 feet wide. The boys rarely wore shoes to school in the summertime, hence their dilemma: how to cross the thistle patches in bare feet. The option of taking the long way around and avoiding the thistles was quickly over-ruled. The only other option was to back up and run as fast as possible through the narrowest part.

"I can still vividly remember the experience," Roy writes, "running full speed in bare feet across 20 feet of prickly thistles, yelping in pain all the way. When the three of us reached the black soil on the other side, we would immediately hit the dirt and start pulling out the few thistle ends that stuck in our feet. 'I had four briars get me—how many did you get?' was a sample of our post-agony conversation."

Sometimes we approach transition in the same way these boys approached the thistle patch. We reason, "If we can get through the process as quickly as possible, perhaps the pain will be minimized." Such an approach would be fine if it worked, but it rarely does.

Some of us try to deny the pain by spending all of our time listening to others tell us how they feel instead of giving adequate attention to our own thoughts and feelings. A pastor may feel more "noble" ministering to his people than dealing with his own "termination emotions." Yet he may be harming himself psychologically. It's healthier for everyone if the pastor talks openly about what he is going through emotionally and spiritually as he leaves a parish. The direct and honest approach will enable him to be more open to what others in the parish are experiencing.

Parish communities have their own ways of denying that their pastor is leaving. Sometimes parishioners refuse to talk about the termination among themselves. They avoid making plans related to the leaving such as setting a date for a farewell. Or they procrastinate in organizing a search committee to determine the church's needs and qualifications for the new minister. In one parish, denial mixed with anger expressed itself when parishioners failed to plan a welcome get-together for the new pastor. After four months, a welcome was finally arranged as part of a potluck supper. Understandably, the pastor reacted negatively.

"I'm furious!"

After moving through denial, those in the dying process usually enter a time of anger, according to Kubler-Ross. During a pastoral transition, we become angry because we sense we are losing something valuable or someone highly prized or greatly treasured. The loss could include friends, an accepting Christian community, or a favorable environment.

In some parishes, anger is expressed indirectly: for example, instead of seeking a new pastor, parishioners may ask an associate pastor to take over the responsibilities of the person who has left. The people's experience of church will not have to change very much; it may seem as if the pastor has simply gone on vacation. In this case, an innocent person—the associate pastor—may bear the brunt of anger that should have been directed elsewhere.

The individual leaving the community also experiences angry feelings which, if not expressed, can backfire later on. One pastor left a parish after being confronted about his drinking problem. In his new parish, he remained aloof from his parishioners, isolating himself until the whole church community was alienated. Having never forgiven his previous parish for confronting him, this pastor spent a great deal of time and energy being angry and bitter.

To deal adequately with angry feelings it may be appropriate for the person leaving to consult a spiritual director, a trained counselor, or a trusted friend with a listening ear. Sharing hostility about the situation with persons involved in the decision—the bishop or church official, a personnel committee, or a group of individuals in the parish or institution—may also help clear the air. The pastor should also consider dealing directly and candidly with those against whom he/she harbors a grudge—perhaps a staff member or volunteer, a choir director, or parishioner who has a different view of what the church means today. If some kind of reconciliation can be achieved, the individual will have subtracted a heavy weight from his soul and will feel free from the past.

When leaving one parish where I served as pastor, I sought to ritualize the reconciliation process. At the beginning of the regular Sunday liturgy, I asked the congregation to call to mind any instances in which they felt I had hurt them or treated them unfairly. After a few moments of silence, I then asked forgiveness of them for my words or actions. Next I paused briefly and asked them to reflect about the times they may have dealt with me unfairly. Following this, I assured them of my forgiveness. We concluded the process by praying together a common prayer of contrition, asking God's merciful forgiveness on all of us. After the service, we felt a certain closure and a willingness to begin to look to the future.

"Isn't there some other way?"

In the third phase of the dying process we begin to bargain. In a church transition, the pastor may delay leaving and begin to reconsider the decision. He may try to make up for past shortcomings and failures: he'll complete an unfinished project, update the bookkeeping, visit the sick or shut-ins who had been neglected.

The parishioners also have their way of bargaining. They may petition the bishop or church official to retain the pastor in his position. Or they may invite the pastor to dinner or express their appreciation in other ways, hoping that he will change his mind and stay.

"It's really going to happen."

Resignation, the next stage in the termination process, can be described as a sense of loss characterized by sadness or depression. If there has been any depth to the relationships that are about to be changed dramatically, there will be sad feelings. It may not be realistic at this stage to try to cheer people up.

A pastor may find he has no sense of direction and feel weighed down also by guilt for past failures in ministry. At times of leaving, all those situations we wish we had handled differently come back to haunt us: inappropriate remarks made in sermons; insensitivity to people at weddings or funerals; decisions made too fast; impatience with those whose pace or lifestyle are different; indifference to women's issues or the role of the laity in the church.

During this time, the pastor may also come to a deeper realization of the real love that the parishioners have felt for him. Positive thoughts and feelings never before expressed now come to the surface and the parish environment suddenly seems less hostile, more comfortable. The pastor may feel very sad about leaving it behind. It's comforting to realize that Jesus himself experienced this kind of sadness. In the Garden of Gethsemane, he lamented his impending death, but also certainly the loss of his friends and those he loved.

Parishioners, too, experience the normal sad feelings of impending loss. They remember how the pastor celebrated the baptism of a child, was instrumental in bringing someone back into the church, officiated at the wedding of a son or a daughter, or offered support at the death of a loved one. Some individuals may also feel guilt at their failure to support and encourage the pastor during his time in the parish. Perhaps they neglected to acknowledge when good was being accomplished, and remained silent when support was needed most.

During this stage there's much looking back and often an inability to maintain a sense of direction. Some will be unwilling to make plans for the new minister. Many activities, from painting the church to ordering Sunday School materials, will be put "on hold" until the new pastor arrives.

"Let's move on now."

The final stage of the dying process is acceptance—letting go of the past with reluctance and anticipating the future with some degree of hope. At this point positive movement begins to occur. The pastor who is leaving experiences a growing feeling of satisfaction about the good that has been accomplished. He realizes anew that no one is indispensable. The church will go on without him. We are all pilgrim people in this world and must move on.

During this time of acceptance, the pastor may be challenged to acknowledge his limitations in ministry and appreciate the variety of gifts given to others. He may say, "Yes, it is time for someone new to come and fill up the gaps left by my own ministry in this church."

The parish also begins to take a new direction. Parishioners make plans to say goodbye gracefully. Leaders in the church suggest sensitive and creative ways of expressing appreciation to the pastor who is leaving. People become more willing to assess the needs of the parish. And as they sense a renewed responsibility to continue the good work that has begun, they look forward to welcoming a new pastor into their midst. When parishioners begin to look ahead with enthusiasm, it indicates that they have gracefully passed through the stages of dying and letting go. For such a community, the best is yet to come.

Romans 6:5 reads, "If we have been united with him through likeness to his death, so shall we be through a like resurrection." Only as we live through the Good Fridays of our lives can we begin to embrace the reality of Easter. Yet for many of us, resurrection images are difficult to capture. Martha and Mary had a similar struggle. In John 11:23-26 Jesus assures the sisters, "Your brother will rise again."

"I know he will rise again," Martha replied, "in the resurrection on the last day."

Jesus then replied, "I am the resurrection and the life; whoever believes in me, though he should die, will come to life; and whoever is alive and believes in me will never die. Do you believe this?"

If we have gone through a traumatic transition process, we may hesitate in answering that last question. Yet Christ's example assures us that it is possible to move beyond the dying to a place of new life, enthusiasm, and hope.

The Next Chapter: Starting Over Again

Certain attitudes and approaches can help accomplish an effective transition. It is important for the new pastor to avoid comparisons between the previous assignment and the present situation. This is similar to someone in a second marriage comparing his current spouse to his former one. Most people would react negatively to such a comparison.

Instead, the new church person would do well to listen carefully to the various groups to discover the needs of the community. It takes time to build trust and establish relationships with these individuals and groups. Now is a good time for the pastor to focus his dreams and life direction. As the Old Testament proverb tells us, "If people have no dreams, they perish." As he becomes focused, he will escape the folly of trying to be all things to all people.

While focusing dreams, it may be necessary to clarify expectations, both the pastor's and the parishioners'. Much misunderstanding and hurt results when expectations—not clear to begin with—are not met. Preparing a well-defined job description for the pastor is a good step in the right direction.

Parishioners will also be wise to avoid making comparisons between the former pastor and the new one. Comparing makes it more difficult to recognize and affirm the special talents of the new person. During this start-up time, parishioners might do well to focus their dreams. What areas of the parish need special attention? What are the opportunities and obstacles to further growth?

The transition will proceed well only if a number of people are willing to take the responsibility for seeing that it happens. I recommend forming a transition team of people from the local community along with representatives from the larger church assembly, such as the bishop or designated church official. It is important that the pastor feel acceptance and support from these people and understand clearly from the bishop the expectations in the new ministry setting. If he is expected to build a new church, solve financial problems, work with inactive members, or simply "see if you can get those people going"? The congregation should also be aware of these expectations so that misunderstandings can be avoided.

To insure a positive start-up, the transition team should take responsibility for several tasks:

1) Help the new pastor move in and get settled. Arrange for an orientation to the facilities, office, and current parish procedures. Things that look simple to old-timers may bewilder someone new.

2) Plan the formal welcome or installation ceremony. When the beginning of a ministry is ritualized, its importance may be more fully appreciated. Make sure parishioners in each of the worship services are involved.

3) Introduce the pastor to the congregation and leaders of the community. Some people are gregarious and outgoing, while others find meeting new people difficult. Having a local person help with introductions can greatly speed up the welcoming process.

In several rural parishes where I served, I began by asking local people to take me to visit parishioners. Each day someone would arrive with a list of people to see and drive me right to the farm, ward off all unfriendly dogs, and introduce me to the family. We only stayed for about a half an hour, but I met lots of people. I did not remember all of them immediately, but they remembered that I had taken the time to visit their home.

The work of the transition team should continue for at least six months after the new person arrives. Thereafter periodic checkups should be enough to ward off problems. Perhaps the bishop or church leader could call or drop a note asking how everything is going. The parish staff could also set aside a brief time to check signals with the new pastor. There may still be grieving to be done about the change. The transition team could take the responsibility for these checkups, which will surely be perceived by the new pastor as signs of acceptance and support.

Time and attention might also need to be given to the congregation at large. Unfinished grieving sometimes manifests itself in defensiveness, resentment, or hostility. Dealing with these reactions at an early stage may ward off an "ecclesiastical shoot-out" down the road.

The parish staff also plays a key role in helping the pastor adjust to a new environment. They can do much to minimize stress and provide for continuity. Staff members serve as public relations people within the larger church community. When parishioners ask,

"What is the new pastor like?", the staff person's answer will influence a happy or unhappy start-up.

Yet the arrival of a new pastor can be threatening to present staff people as they wonder, "Will I be able to work with the new pastor?" Some of this stress can be minimized by consulting the staff during the hiring process. If they perceive the new person's arrival as an opportunity for growth, then all concerned will be winners.

Indeed, all of us—parishioners, staff, pastor—*can* grow spiritually during a transition if we are able to translate the dying and rising of Christ into practical terms. Transitions are part of the human experience. We need to learn how to say hello and goodbye. If we can do both gracefully, then we truly will have followed in the footsteps of the Risen Christ.

NOTES

1. This article deals with the transition process as it relates to churches and church personnel. The term "pastor" is used throughout for the sake of uniformity; the principles, however, apply in various settings. Please substitute other titles, such as pastoral minister, associate, or staff person—either male or female—as appropriate.

2. Elisabeth Kubler-Ross, *On Death and Dying* (New York: Macmillan Publishing Co., Inc., 1969).

3. Roy M. Oswald, *Running Through the Thistles*, (Washington, DC: The Alban Institute, 1978).

PART IV

Special Goodbyes

Saying "goodbye" at retirement can be especially poignant because retirement itself is often a traumatic transition, especially for those clergy who have been addicted to their work.

If my identity is too much wrapped up in my role, who am I after I retire?

In "Saying Goodbye To My Parish" Hugh Peniston describes the process by which he ended a pastorate of 33 years. Using Roy Oswald's book *Running Through The Thistles*,[1] Hugh stretched his farewell over a year's time.

Interim pastors say goodbye frequently, and often shortly after they have said hello. Alice Martin describes some of her learnings and mixed emotions as she finished a one-year interim in a congregation that was still seeking a pastor.

Probably the most difficult setting in which to say goodbye is when the congregation itself is closing.

Congregations die with great difficulty. There is often a tenacious loyalty on the part of a loyal remnant who resist the demise of a cherished community of faith that contains their story. Our Presbytery delayed the dissolution of a congregation for three full years because the five remaining members were adamantly opposed.

In such a case the members of the congregation are not saying goodbye to the pastor with the expectation of making a new beginning. The congregation is saying goodbye to the pastor and to its own life simultaneously.

In "When A Church Dies" Daphne Burt describes the importance of being vulnerable and sharing the pain of the flock.

NOTES

1. (Washington, DC: The Alban Institute, 1978).

Saying Goodbye to My Parish

by D. Hugh Peniston

Recently I brought to a close a ministry of some thirty-three years in this community, having decided to spend the next few years before I *really* retire developing a specialized ministry in helping churches to build and manage housing projects. Naturally such a decision took a lot of thought on my part, and the actual discussions with the personnel committee about this step took place over a period of more than a year. My associate, who was on a temporary part-time contract, left at the same time I did, December 31, 1979.

During the period of planning I read the book *Running Through the Thistles*[1] several times, and very carefully. I had my associate read it, too, and asked him to be my counselor as I worked at this termination process. Later on I reviewed the book carefully with our governing board, the Session, where we talked about the process and how we were all doing with it at more than one meeting. The book was extremely helpful to us, and I want to express my deep appreciation for it. I would like to share some observations about this experience.

We had in our church a much longer time to deal with the termination than most churches have available. The Session knew about the decision a full year before it happened. The people on the personnel group knew about it about six months ahead of time, although the exact date was not set until the fall.

Because of the time available, we did a lot of planning, preparing for the interim period, creating and training task forces, doing a careful study of the mission of the church, and taking care of all the matters involved in the change.

I found that this planning soon involved me in one of the most creative periods of my long ministry. It also insured my total involvement in being the pastor of the church until the last day. I created a special countdown calendar that had a sheet for each day remaining in my ministry. I started this with the number 93 and would tear off a page each day. This reminded me of the urgency of the tasks still to be done. Everyone on the Session saw this calendar, and members of the congregation knew of it. On the last day, December 31st, it seemed important to me to work in my office until midnight, after which I tore off the last page numbered "1."

This calendar became an important part of my own grief process. At first I found it an amusing exercise. In time I came to hate the calendar and wanted to destroy it, for there was too much pain by then in pulling off the sheets. I went through emotions of anger and disbelief as the numbers got lower. In time this gave way to resignation and then acceptance. I noted the close parallel with the emotions of the dying patient. In fact, at the meeting where a pastor seeking committee was chosen I commented, "I feel like a man dying in the hospital, who has just told his wife it's all right if she marries again after he's gone."

A denominational official made one comment to me that seemed to me to show a lack of sensitivity. When I handed him the resolution adopted by the congregation agreeing to the termination, he remarked, "So, you are now a lame duck pastor." It was a matter of great pride to me, and important in the process, that I was truly the pastor of the church until midnight the last day.

When the termination date was only a month off and I realized all that remained to be done, and how the events of the Christmas season would interfere with plans for final calls for me and for parishioners, I decided to write letters to people who had given special support and friendship over the years.

Each of these letters I wrote in longhand, reliving first in my mind all of the experiences I had had with that person and the family over these many years. The letters seemed very hard to get started on as each one required first this mental effort, but many things came back to me, and I felt good about these letters when they were completed. While I did make calls, the letters seemed to me more consistent with my style of dealing with deep things.

A number of these letters were to people with whom I had had conflict. I spoke of these tensions frankly in the letters. These often led to important interactions. For example, one woman, who had been the leader of a move to have me leave some nine years ago, embraced me after church the following Sunday, thanked me for the letter and said, "I wept when I read it. I am so glad you wrote it."

What was ironic about my letter writing program was that the congregation had decided to surprise me at the farewell dinner with a memory book composed of letters that people in the congregation wrote me. In these letters families reviewed their experiences with me over the years. It was revealing to me to see how events, many of which I had forgotten, looked from their perspective. What seemed to me important was that members of the congregation were given a definite way of working on their grief process that involved the same reliving process that had been helpful to me.

This process reminded me of what happened when my father died. I had returned to the home I grew up in for the funeral, and afterwards I helped my mother with details. But most important to me was spending several days cleaning the cellar. Each tool or discarded project reminded me of things I had done with my father long ago as a child. Over the days I worked there (there was a lot to clean out for he hadn't thrown anything away!), I relived my entire life with my father. When the last load of things was taken away I felt that somehow a great task was completed. My grief work was done.

So it was after the farewell dinner. I found it was almost too painful to read the letters. I forced myself to do it however, a few every day, until I was finished. Then I had a similar feeling of a task being done. I will read the letters again in the future, but it will be different.

During the last month I was conscious of doing many things for the last time. I used the sermon time each Sunday to speak of what I had learned in our years together and what we had stood for. They seemed to me, and to others, some of the best sermons I had done. Also, we did considerable entertaining. We had an open house Christmas Sunday to which a large number of good friends came. We had a dinner for the Session before our last meeting together. On some of these last occasions we talked about what it had all meant. There was warmth, laughter, and deep emotion.

On my last Sundays there were special events, the reception of new members and baptisms, which people wanted to get done before I left. On the Sunday before my last Sunday we had a party after church for my associate. He felt it important to separate his going from mine. On my last Sunday I did the service alone, as I had done it most of those 33 years.

In response to a suggestion in the book *Running Though the Thistles*,[1] I prepared a service of termination, picking up the theme of the last hymn, "O God Our Help in Ages Past," a hymn connected with other experiences in my life.

On that evening a farewell dinner was held. This was a warm and happy event, with much good humor. It was more of a celebration than a farewell, although there were times of deep emotion and some tears. Friends spoke of various aspects of my ministry. My own family presented a slide show of my ministry with my wife and my children participating. The children had come home for this affair. The slide show and their participation were a surprise to me.

Not only the good times, but some of the difficult times in my ministry were referred to in this dinner. This seemed to me important.

I have written far more than I intended about this. Perhaps it may be useful to you in some way. We worked very hard at going through the termination process creatively. The result is that the congregation now is working energetically and with excitement at the interim tasks. Even before we came to the last day, good friends said, "Yes, it is hard, but it is challenging and exciting, too."

Recently when members of a presbytery team met with the core group of Session members they came away amazed at how our people "had it all together." The leaders of the church are eager to get on with new tasks, feel confident about themselves, and good about our church. "We have nothing to apologize for to anyone," they seemed to be saying. "We are doing a good job. We know where we are going."

NOTE

1. Roy Oswald, *Running Through the Thistles* (Washington, DC: The Alban Institute, 1978).

How Do We Say Goodbye?

by Alice Martin

"I'm not going to get attached to this preacher. I'm not even invit-
ing her to my house and then have her break my heart again when
she leaves like the other pastors." That is what an 80-year-old member of the congregation told me and others when I first came to
Reisterstown. Now, after I have had several visits and meals in her
home, she says, "I think I'm closer to her than any of the others
and I know I'll cry just as much, if not more, when she leaves."

People getting involved and sharing their lives with each other
is an unavoidable and important aspect of ministry, and makes the
pain of separation inevitable. The interim ministry is particularly
hazardous in this respect because the pastor enters knowing that in
a few months, or perhaps a year, the relationship will be severed.

The goodbye process starts from the beginning. Some people
say, "You can't get close, or make long-range plans," "One year is
too short a time," "We didn't have high expectations of her or ourselves." But that process provides the opportunity for developing interdependence rather than dependence. One of the real temptations
that I have felt and that has been identified by other interims is "the
temptation of the interim pastor to restore trust *in the interim pastor* on a kind of personalistic basis, which leaves the congregation
doubly bereft when he or she leaves."

Before I had found a new job and while they were encountering
disappointments and rejection as they searched for a new pastor,
there were times when I was tempted to stay. After I found my new
job, I began to have guilt feelings about leaving. I could not reassure them of their value as a congregation when I, like so many
others, was going to desert them. They must have sensed my guilt
because I was continually asked why I would not stay, even though
I remained firm in my commitment of only one year.

The guilt, denial, and depression became significant aspects of our saying goodbye. That grieving process made it difficult for me to admit to them that we have differences as well as similarities and that those differences are pulling us in separate directions of growth. I have been reluctant to say that I go with joy as well as with sadness, and I have not really wanted to hear them admit that they, too, will have some feelings of relief when I leave. I have had to remind myself continually that the interim is a time to help a congregation learn to live in faith by letting go of the past, and that means letting go of the interim pastor.

It is difficult for me to leave, especially because at this point the church has not achieved its major goal of finding a new pastor. But I see signs of hope that I want them to recognize before I go.

Interviews with my lay training committee were one way to help members of the congregation examine some of the changes that have taken place during the year. Reviewing goals with the commissions and the board, talking about what has happened and what they would like to accomplish in the future, raising the question of whether and/or how the Bible study group plans to continue, a special dedication of the storage shed (if it is finished), some concluding sermons that reflect back over the changes the year has brought, and a ritual for saying goodbye developed jointly with the Ministry Commission and used during the final worship service— these are all ways of saying goodbye that I will suggest. I am sure that in the spirit of the Free Church there will also be tears and other unplanned expressions of "goodbye." My major hope as I leave and hear, as some are already saying, "You have a good future before you," is that I can turn and say, "So do you."

When a Church Dies:
A Pastor's Perspective

by Daphne Burt

On Sunday April 5, 1987, I preached to four people. The offering that Sunday almost equalled the regular offering when all the members worshipped. I may have had some idea of the status of the parish before that time, but after the 5th of April, I had no doubt. Christ Lutheran Church of Bristol, Tennessee wasn't just on its last legs; it was dead.

My ministry to this dying congregation taught me a special sensitivity and care which led me to conclude that ministry to such a parish is not essentially different from that to a growing, healthy church. Perhaps the most important realization for me was that I need to bring in my presence and person the Good News that pain and suffering are not the last word, that all people are loved, forgiven, redeemed, and promised resurrection. What happened to me physically and emotionally leads me to believe that I was called to embody the hurt and misery of the people I served. This was very difficult. I felt at times like a dog's prey, shaken and played with before being put out of its misery. It is much easier to bring Good News without being touched by the pain and suffering needed to bring it to birth. However, my ministry began to be fruitful only when I stopped trying to be in control and allowed the experience of the dying church to affect me deeply. This is the reality of the "Wounded Healer." Henri Nouwen remarks:

> No one can help anyone without becoming involved, without entering with his (sic) whole person into the painful situation, without taking the risk of being hurt, wounded, or even destroyed in the process. The beginning and end of all Christian leadership is to give your life for others.[1]

It was only when I allowed the pain of closing Christ Church to touch me that I was able to touch and deal with the pain of the people I was called to serve.

When I realized that the church would close, I had grand ideas of what I would do for the people. I would help them come to terms with this devastating event by making sure that we talked about it—often. I would provide opportunities for them to emote. My agenda included being sure that they left Christ Church with a strong sense of Lutheran identity and heritage. It was an exercise in futility. I was asking my people to learn new things when they were burned out by having hung on to the old. The problem was that as I objectified the experience with programmatic goals, I put more distance between myself and the congregation. The people of Christ Church did not need me to do for them, they needed me to be with them.

As the months progressed, my sermons suffered. In an attempt to recharge my preaching batteries, I attended a lecture at Lutheran Theological Southern Seminary by Elizabeth Achtemeier. She emphasized that pastors should always "tell the story," and I realized then that while I had been intent upon preaching theologically sound sermons, I was leaving out my own experience. By so doing, I was giving the congregation permission to leave their stories out of the Good News of God's love as well.

Finally, my desire to stay in control of what was truly a disaster in the life of the congregation meant that I refused to show how much I was affected by what was occurring. I never cried publicly and this was especially confusing to Church Council members who were extremely close to the situation and were unable to make it through a meeting without some tears. My intentional control of emotion was difficult for them to understand. Was it all right for them to cry if their pastor did not?

My need for control had other manifestations as well. I found that one of the most difficult aspects of closing out the ministry of the congregation was the decreased activity and work requirements. As someone who likes to keep active and busy, I felt quite guilty about my forced inactivity, and I did not know how to handle either the guilt or the lack of things to do. I did not understand at the time that the congregation was experiencing the same thing. They too were used to taking part in many projects and programs. While they were still busy with immediate needs such as church maintenance, their other involvements were significantly reduced. I would have been far more effective had I used my own guilt to interpret and relate to theirs.

My behavior during the first few months of ministry after having realized that the congregation was indeed dying was marked by my desire to escape the feelings, effects, and implications of what was happening. By my avoidance, I allowed the congregation to dodge the experience as well. Pastor and parish were colluding in evading the pain.

The turning point for me was when I realized that I wasn't functioning very well. I had trouble eating and sleeping. Seeking help from the synod psychologist, I was diagnosed as having a classic case of depression and medication was prescribed. This was a shock to me. Suddenly I had to face the fact that I could not go it alone, that pastoring a dying church was not just a challenging ministry that I could perform adequately, but one which deeply affected my entire life. I could no longer afford to pretend to be untouched.

The following Sunday, I preached again the sermon I had written for April 5. This time I had a "full" congregation of thirteen. As I modified some of the Lenten themes of the sermon, I also added my own experience. "Have you ever been depressed?" I asked. "Well, I know what it feels like because I have just been diagnosed as being chemically depressed." This was extremely difficult to admit publicly, especially from the pulpit, but it seemed essential that I do so. As I spoke of my own depression, I was able to address the fact that the entire congregation was depressed. It seemed that for the first time we were on the same journey together, acknowledging the fact that none of us was unmoved by the experience.

From that point on it was easier for me to share my own pain about what was happening to the parish. I still was not able to cry at Council meetings, but members believed me when I confessed that I cried copious tears at home. The trust level in our relationship increased dramatically as it became clear to all that I was there not just to manage the organizational details of closing down the church, but I was there to be with a suffering people and to suffer with them.

We began to share many of the effects of the impending death. All of us felt increasingly overwhelmed by what was happening. Although the Synod had encouraged us to make the decision to disband on our own terms, we all felt that the closure was something happening to us, and really out of our control. I related strongly to this feeling; I had had a choice in accepting the call but, never having closed a church before, had no idea how painful it would be. I felt misled in not having been warned about how difficult such a call would necessarily be. Over and over again parishioners told me that it was not my fault that the church was closing. Only later did I realize that I needed to have repeated those words back to them. It was not their fault either.

As I became aware of my own depression, I had a great need to take better care of myself. I did this by spending a lot of time out of town with friends; by the last month I was out of the parish three to four days a week. Much of my need to do this was still escapism, but the results were far more healthy than moping around the parsonage. Again, my actions gave meaning and permission to those of the parishioners; even the most active members who had previously made a point of never being out of town because they knew their presence was vital began to take vacations and "Sunday off." I found that I did not resent these planned absences because I fully understood the motivation and need for them.

As we approached closure, we continued to mirror each other's experiences. I had placed a great deal of emphasis on their continuing their fine ministry in other local Lutheran churches. This began to be acceptable to them only when I also began to speak about my own prospects for a new call. They were as concerned about my vocation continuing as I was about theirs.

We spoke constantly about our desire to celebrate our last worship service with joy and hope. We planned a picnic and some games for the afternoon following the service. Possibly none of us believed that we would really be able to be joyful on a Sunday that we expected would be so full of pain. As it turned out, there were tears, but there was also much laughter. I was relieved and relaxed, and it would appear that the rest of the congregation was able to take their cue from me.

In the end, however, I did not allow myself to say goodbye. By so doing, I circumvented that last most essential act of dealing with the death of the congregation. Upon reflection, I could have said goodbye by having had the courage to openly embrace the suffering I would endure, knowing that I would not be alone in that suffering. I had not done this consistently, however. I chose to preach one more "good theological sermon." It would have been preferable to share my personal reflections and remembrances. Because I said goodbye inadequately, much of the congregation did not feel very free to deal with the significant pain of the congregational family separating and the inevitability of losing touch with those who had been important in their lives for years. Because their pastor had not said goodbye, the congregation was disabled from saying goodbye as well.

An extremely meaningful event did occur during the final worship service which may have offset my not having said goodbye in a direct fashion. We had planned a time of extemporaneous thanksgiving prayer, not knowing whether anyone would feel comfortable praying out loud. As it turned out, many of the visitors at the service, former members of Christ Church, prayed for us. Christ Church parishioners were unable to speak because of their tears, and so it was a moment when they received a powerful expression of love and care without having to return it.

I was able to take this time of prayer to speak of my love for the congregation. I closed my prayer with the words, "I have learned from all of you that being a pastor does not just mean being able to love, it also means being able to be loved." Perhaps I had been able to say goodbye after all.

A pastor embodies and enfleshes the Good News that all people are loved, forgiven, redeemed, and given new life by God, no matter what their experiences or life stories are. My ministry to the death of Christ Church reminded me that as I am called to encounter my own pain and suffering, I am able to give meaning and permission to the people of God to do the same without fear.

It was a painful but God-filled time for us all. We were able to experience in a very personal fashion what it means to live out Christ's death and resurrection. Christ Church truly died, but its people and pastor were given new life and look forward to participating in Christ's Church in new places.

NOTE

1. Henri J. M. Nouwen, *The Wounded Healer: Ministry in Contemporary Society* (Garden City, NY: Doubleday & Co., Inc., 1972).

PART V

Liturgical Resources
for the Closure
of the Pastoral Relationship

Most important transitions in life are expressed in liturgy, whether it be baptism, confirmation, marriage, or death. There have been recent liturgies to enable a couple to acknowledge the experience of divorce. Worship can help us make transitions.

This section contains a model liturgy and a litany. Both were adapted from Episcopal sources for ecumenical use.

A Service for the Ending of a Pastoral Relationship

(This service is modeled after an Episcopal Service and has been revised for ecumenical use.)

Service of the Word

An opening hymn may be sung. The people stand.

Celebrant: Blessed be God, Creator, Redeemer, and Holy Spirit.

People: Blessed be God's reign, now and forever. Amen.

Celebrant: There is one Body and one Spirit;

People: There is one hope in God's call to us;

Celebrant: One Lord, one Faith, one Baptism;

People: One God and Parent of all.

Celebrant: The Lord be with you.

People: And also with you.

Celebrant: Let us pray.

Almighty and everlasting God, by whose Spirit the whole body of your faithful people is governed:

Receive our prayers, which we offer to you for all members of your holy Church, that in their ministry they may faithfully serve you.

Direct us, O Lord, in all our doings with your most gracious favor, and further us with your continual help; that in all our works begun, continued, and ended in you, we may glorify your Name.

We pray for the holy catholic Church. Fill it with truth and peace. Where it is corrupt, purify it; where it is in error, direct it; where in anything it is amiss, reform it. Where it is right, strengthen it; where it is in want, provide for it; where it is divided, reunite it; for the sake of Jesus Christ our Lord. Amen.

The Ministry of the Word

Any of the following may be read:

Old Testament
Genesis 31:44-46, 48-49, 50b (The Lord watch between you and me when we are absent one from another)
Genesis 12:1-9 (Abraham's departure from Haran and God's promise to bless him)
Deuteronomy 18:15-18 (God will raise up a prophet like Moses)
Deuteronomy 32:1-9 (The farewell of Moses)
Joshua 24:1, 14-25 (Joshua's farewell to his people)
Ecclesiastes 3:1-7; 7:8, 10, 13-14 (A time for everything; better the end than the beginning)

Epistles
1 Corinthians 3:4-11 (Paul planted, Apollos watered, God gave growth)
Acts 16:9-10 (Paul's call to Macedonia)
Acts 20:17-22, 25-28, 32, 36-38b (Paul's apologia for his ministry at Ephesus)
II Thessalonians 2:13-3:5 (Paul gives thanks for the success of the Gospel)
I Thessalonians 5:12-25 (Paul encourages the ministry among the Thessalonians)
Philippians 4:1-10, 23(Rejoice in the Lord always)

Gospel
Matthew 9:35-38 (The harvest is plentiful but the laborers are few)
Matthew 25:31-40 (As you did it to the least of these you did it to me)
Luke 12:35-38 (The faithful servant)
Luke 17:7-10 (We are unworthy servants; we have only done our duty)
John 10:14-18 (The ministry of the good shepherd)
John 21:15-19 (Feed my sheep)

Sermon
(It may be appropriate for the bishop or church executive to preach the sermon in the course of which a charge should be given to the congregation concerning the nature of ministry.)

Apostles' Creed
The departing pastor then addresses these words to the congregation:

On the ____ day of _____, 19____, I began ministry in this congregation. I have, with God's help and to the best of my abilities exercised this trust.

   After prayer and careful consideration, it now seems to me that I should leave this charge, and I publicly state that my tenure as pastor of this church ends this day.

The pastor may, if desired, briefly state his/her plans for the future. The bishop or executive says:

Do you, the people of _____ , recognize and accept the conclusion of this pastoral relationship?

People: We do.

Then the pastor may express thanksgiving for the time of tenure, with its joys and sorrows, and state hopes for the future of the congregation.

The pastor may present to officers of the congregation a letter of resignation, the keys to the church, or other symbols fitting to the occasion.

The pastor may be joined by members of the family who may want to express what life in the congregation has meant to them.

Representatives of the congregation may wish to respond to the pastor and family, and bid them Godspeed.

The bishop or executive may then indicate what provision has been made for continuation of the ministries of the parish.

The departing pastor and the congregation then say together the following prayer:

O God, you have bound us together for a time as pastor and people to work for the advancement of your kingdom in this place. We give you thanks for the ministry which we have shared in these years now past.
Silence

We thank you for your patience with us despite our blindness and slowness of heart. We thank you for your forgiveness and mercy in the face of our many failures.
Silence

Especially we thank you for your never failing presence with us through these years, and for the deeper knowledge of you and of each other which we have attained.

Silence

We thank you for those who have been joined to this part of Christ's family through baptism. We thank you for opening our hearts and minds again and again to your Word, and for feeding us abundantly with the Sacrament of the Body and Blood of your Son.

Silence

Now, we pray, be with those who leave and with us who stay; and grant that all of us, by drawing nearer to you, may always be close to each other in the communion of saints. All this we ask for the sake of Jesus Christ, your Son, our Lord. Amen

Pastor: The peace of the Lord be always with you.
People: And also with you.

Ministry of the Sacrament

If the Lord's Supper is to follow, the service continues with the offertory.

After the Communion:

People: Almighty God we thank you for feeding us with the Body and Blood of your Son and for uniting us with Him in the fellowship of your Holy Spirit. We thank you for raising up among us faithful servants of your Word and Sacraments. We thank you especially for the work of _____ among us, and the presence of his/her family here. Grant that both he/she and we may serve you in the days ahead, and always rejoice in your glory, and come at length into your heavenly kingdom; through Jesus Christ our Lord. Amen.

Charge and benediction.

A Litany for the Closure of a Ministry

Pastor: On *(date)* _____ we shared together in a service of celebration of a new ministry. It is now time to give thanks for the life we have shared in Christ. It is also time for me to move on to the next chapter in my spiritual journey on which the Lord is leading me.

           I have found our time together rewarding and memories of what we have shared will always remain precious and meaningful.

People: The Lord is loving to everyone;
God's compassion is over all God's works.
All your works praise you, O Lord,
And your faithful servants bless you (Psalm 145:9-10).

Pastor: Let us thank God for what these past years have meant by praying together the General Thanksgiving:

Pastor
and People: Almighty God, Lord of all mercies,
We your unworthy servants give you humble thanks
For all your goodness and loving kindness
To us and to all people.
    We bless you for our creation, preservation, and all
The blessings of this life;
But above all for your incomparable love
In the redemption of the world
By our Lord Jesus Christ;
For the means of grace, and for the hope of glory.
    And we pray,
Give us such an awareness of your mercies
That with truly thankful hearts

> We may make known your praise,
> Not only with our lips, but in our lives,
> By giving up ourselves to your service,
> And by walking before you in holiness and
> Righteousness all our days;
> Through Jesus Christ our Lord, to whom with
> You and the Holy Spirit, be all honor and
> Glory throughout all ages. Amen.

Pastor: Dear friends, you have allowed me to share the responsibilities of the ordained ministry in your midst. At the celebration of a new ministry, you presented me with symbols expressing my special role among you. It is time for me to return to you what you have lent me.

I have tried to proclaim the Word of God faithfully among you. Here is the Bible which expresses this.

The Bible is presented to a lay leader.

People: Thanks be to God.

Pastor: I have shared, through God's grace, in bringing some through the water of new creation into birth into the Body of Christ by Holy Baptism. Here is water which symbolizes God's gift of belonging in Christ.

A vessel of water is given to a lay leader.

People: There is one Body and one Spirit,
There is one Hope in God's call to us.

Pastor: Prayer, both individual and corporate, is the means by which our relationship with God grows, deepens, and strengthens. Here is the *(prayerbook or denominational directory for worship).*

Book is given to a lay leader.

People: Put your trust in God, "for I will yet give thanks to God, for the help of his countenance" (Psalm 42:5)

Pastor: Bread and Wine are the means by which we share in the blessing of Creation and it is the means by which

we offer ourselves to be transformed into the sacramental Body of Christ.

Bread and wine are given to a lay leader.

People: Taste and see that the Lord is good: happy are they
                 who trust in God.

Pastor: And now it is time for me to go forth having restored
                 to you the signs of office which you presented me. I
                 ask that in your love and commitment, you send me
                 forth with a "going away" blessing.

People: Unto God's gracious mercy we commit you.
                 The Lord bless you and keep you;
                 the Lord make his face to shine upon you and be gra-
                     cious unto you.
                 The Lord lift up the light of his countenance upon you
                     and give you peace both this day and forever. Amen.

PART VI

Resources to Help a Congregation Deal with its Feelings and Look to the Future

Sometimes understanding laity can really help the "goodbye process." When the Rev. Sharon Rader left the University United Methodist Church in East Lansing, Michigan to become a District Superintendent, church member Pat Engelmann wrote a letter to the congregation entitled "Just When You Appreciate Them Most . . . They Leave Home." Sharon testifies that many people in the congregation indicated how helpful the letter was to them in gaining a perspective on Sharon's departure.

Also in this section are two sermons. "At Home in the Wilderness" explores the biblical connection between our capacity to say goodbye and our capacity to trust God. It was inspired by the life, ministry, and death of Orville Chadsey, a fine pastor who died after a long struggle with cancer. I have found this sermon especially meaningful to troubled congregations where a pastor has died unexpectedly, or left in the midst of conflict.

"What to Do until the Preacher Comes" is a sequel that explores the opportunities of the transition period in the life of a congregation. I have preached variations of this sermon in many congregations on the Sunday after the departing pastor has left. It provides a frame of reference for the congregation to use in viewing the interim period.

Just When You Appreciate Them Most . . . They Leave Home!

An open letter to the family that is the University United Methodist Church (UUMC)

by Pat Englemann

For some days I've been wrestling with feelings surrounding Sharon's announcement of her promotion to District Superintendent. At some time and place I've felt this way before. The familiar mixture of protest and pride curls around the fringes of my mind as I go about the business of getting through every day. Last night, at that hour when things we don't want to think about creep out to confront us, I began to inspect the beast of my feelings, and at last the comparison became clear. Yes, we certainly *have* been at this juncture before—three times—one for each child who left home. Many of you have also experienced the traumatic juncture of departure—to summer camp, perhaps, or another semester at college—which are sent into our lives to prepare us for the quantum leap of the Children's Growing Up.

The day comes for the Real Job, in preparation for which all that college tuition has been spent—the day of the Wedding comes, or the trip to the airport that must be made with the Independent Person who has decided to take up life half a continent away.

At all these times we're suddenly beset with raging emotion we don't want to acknowledge. These young people have come through all the years of needing nursing through illness, support through school, an eternal listening ear. Just before Lift-Off Day we realize that *now* we *enjoy* talking together. We've just begun to appreciate former dependent children as fascinating adults—but they hear distant signals, and suddenly their lives with us are over, at least on a daily basis.

Well, to be sure, pastors are sent to lead *us*, but there are parallels in the family experience. In a very real sense the congregation interacts to support, encourage, and promote personal growth in much the same way family members relate to each other. When a new pastor arrives, we begin the process of assimilation. We tell the tales of the collective past—the dreams we've achieved, and the failures we've had to swallow. We confess our needs and plan together the directions we'll take, both traditional and covering new ground. We learn to appreciate the strengths of our new leader, and we begin to fit together the puzzle of our shared lives in this place and at this new time.

Over months we get to know the pastor as a loving, guiding person, and we give thanks for talents brought to us. We begin to let our individual guard down, and admit that we are less than perfect, even in our own protective eyes. A very comfortable relationship is in the weaving at this point. We are feeling at home, and the family of UUMC is once again confident and content.

Then, often without warning to most of us, the hand of fate we call The Conference decides our pastor's talents are sorely needed in some new venture. Our leader is snatched—uprooted—from our congregational family, and many of us are devastated. The blow comes just when all was going so well—new programs thriving, wonderful new people coming into the fellowship, above all the Home Folks feeling is warming us and helping us reach out and do for others in ways we might have shunned in less secure days.

Nobody embraces loss eagerly; not one of us willingly watches a good friend depart. Yet we don't have a vote in this decision, just as we really don't have a say when those kids hear their distant drums . . . or fall in love . . . or find a perfect job in Australia.

When family members leave us, though, life does go on. There *is* life after high school, after college, after the kids are married and settled half a continent away. The cornerstone of many lives in our realm of Methodism is the *congregation* headquartered in UUMC. The congregation is our extended family, whom we help, by whom we are cheered and encouraged, and with whom we share our tears and laughter. We're still here for each other. When pastors change—still the Home Place survives.

UUMC is unique among Methodist churches. Because of our proximity to a great university campus and a state capitol, marvelous talent comes to us—and just as quickly leaves us. We have many, many people with leadership skills—at times it might be better to have a few more "Indians" and not quite such a preponderance of "chiefs!" But that's the way we are, and have always been. We say "goodbye" more often to congregation members than any church in most of our prior experience. We are known as a "difficult" congregation because we *are* always changing. Our high-speed turnover and great diversity generates a dynamism that can be felt. To pastors coming in, we often seem like the "refiner's fire," and test them sorely by our unpredictability and constant shift of personnel.

Along with the pain we feel with the way we are and the friends we lose so quickly, we also receive great blessings as a group. Young people come to us in their school days and the difficult years of starting homes and families; many come from countries far away. Young pastors also come just out of the seminary. They all leave, as they must, but they are changed by being here, and they take a little spark of the UUMC spirit to light fires in their new lives thousands of miles away.

Our deep affection and pride travels with our far-flung UUMC family, just as it accompanies our own grown children. We do not forget them, and we rejoice when news reaches us of their good fortune. All over the world live lay persons and pastors who were once part of UUMC, and in a very real sense they are still "part of the family." For them, for ourselves, and for the future lives destined to touch our own, we must keep true to our purpose.

We admit—wearily, at times—that it's time to struggle and grow again. That's what we're here for. *We* are the *family* of UUMC. Our very new sister, Sharon, must leave, and we don't want her to do that just now. When we turn away from self and consider Sharon, we know that this uprooting is just as keenly felt by her and her family. Obeying her vows as an ordained Methodist minister, she is trying to ready herself to go where she has been asked to serve. She needs our loving support right now just as each of our children do when they heed their call to leave home.

And, somewhere soon, a new pastor will be hearing about an assignment to East Lansing. Maybe our reputation will travel before us and a bit of dread will begin to creep into that life.

Certainly, somewhere, someone will also be saying "goodbye" to a very dear church family and setting off to the unknown future of our lives together.

A new chapter in the UUMC family history will soon begin. We want it to be another very good chapter. We have many new members of the congregation family to nurture and bond in fellowship. Sharon has given us much love and very good leadership. We want to build on that.

I cry when those airplanes lift off, every time; but then it's time to get on with my life here, and look to tomorrow with hope, expectation, and love!

At Home in the Wilderness:
A Sermon on Saying Goodbye

by Edward A. White

Have you ever been lost in the wilderness?

It's not like being lost in civilization. Generally when we get lost
in the city, it's a nuisance. We have to call for directions and retrace
our steps. It's embarrassing when we walk in 20 minutes late for
the meeting.

But when you get lost in the wilderness, your very life can be at
stake.

The closest I've come to it is to be lost at sea in a small boat in
the fog ... without a compass. After a time of considerable anxiety I
picked up the sound of a friendly fog horn off Brenton Reef, Rhode
Island. Were it not for that fog horn I might yet be drifting in the
North Atlantic.

It's a scary thing to be lost in the wilderness!

That's what the Hebrew people found out.

At first they were thrilled to be delivered from slavery in Egypt.
But when they got out there into the Sinai desert, and ran out of
food and water, they let Moses know in no uncertain terms that it
would have been better to remain slaves in Egypt than to come out
into the wilderness to die.

And yet it was precisely there in the wilderness that the Hebrew
people learned for the first time what it really meant to trust God,
one day at a time, for food and water.

And it was precisely when the people were leaving the wilderness
to enter the Promised Land that God became worried about them. In
Deuteronomy 8 God says, in effect, "I'm giving you a land flowing
with milk and honey and cattle and crops and silver and gold. . . . But
I'm worried about what will happen to you when you get all these
goodies. I'm afraid you will forget how to trust me. I'm afraid you will
become puffed up in your hearts and say to yourselves, 'My power
and the might of my hand have gotten me this wealth!' "

"And," says the Lord, "if you ever come to that conclusion, you will surely perish!"

And sure enough, that's exactly what happened.

The wilderness is a scary place.

Everything is unpredictable in the wilderness.

We are not in control.

There are many dangers and we are very vulnerable.

That is why the human race constantly tries to escape from the wilderness. Ever since the Tower of Babel we human beings have tried to build cities and to create civilization to escape from the wilderness. We want a world that is predictable and where we can be in control . . . where we can push buttons and turn switches . . . to go where *we* want to go and do what *we* want to do, according to our own schedule. Above all, we want to be insulated from risk, danger, and pain.

The only trouble is, we never quite succeed.

No matter how hard we try to create a safe, predictable world where we can be in control, the wilderness keeps invading our lives.

Consider your own pilgrimage through life.

Being born has to be a wilderness experience. None of us remembers it, but surely when we were first born we weren't in control of anything. We were totally dependent on others for our survival.

As we grew older we gradually began, through trial and error, to take responsibility for our lives. Life began to be somewhat predictable, and we began to feel somewhat in control.

Then, for many, though not all, comes the experience euphemistically referred to as "falling in love." "Falling" is a good term because when you're falling you aren't in control of anything. At first it's a "warm fuzzy," but after the honeymoon is over you discover that there is someone else on the other end of the line now who has a mind and will of their own. That nice predictable world where you were in control is constantly being interrupted.

Those early years of marriage can be a true wilderness experience of pain and unpredictability. If you work at it, however, and if you are lucky, you may begin together to create a life that is somewhat predictable and where together you feel somewhat in control.

Then along come children, and the uncertainty of the wilderness invades our lives again. If there's anything in this world that is unpredictable, it's kids.

Two of my favorite songs are from the musical *The Fantasticks*. Two fathers sing together about what it's like to raise children:

Why do the kids put beans in their ears?
No one can hear with beans in their ears.
After a while the reason appears.
They did it 'cause we said 'No!'[1]

or again:

Plant a radish, get a radish, not a brussels sprout.
That's why I like vegetables; you know what you're about.[2]

Vegetables are predictable; "childerin are bewilderin'." Yet if
we're lucky, and if we work at it, we endure the unpredictability
and risk of raising children. Gradually, through trial and error, they
learn to take responsibility for their lives, and they move up and
out into the world.

Now we enter the "era of the empty nest." Now at last we can
have a quiet, civilized, predictable life where we are in control.
Right?

Wrong! Now we begin to experience that phenomenon called
"aging." We discover that we are not even in control of our own
bodies the way we used to be.

Again the wilderness invades our lives. And the final invasion is
the experience of death—death of those we love, and finally our
own. None of us has control over that.

The moral of the story is that no matter how hard we try, we
cannot escape the wilderness. We can never have a world where we
are in control, where we are secure from danger, and where there
is no uncertainty.

This is the point of Jesus' temptation in the wilderness.

According to the story, Jesus was led by the Holy Spirit into the
wilderness to be tempted by the devil. And then there is that mas-
terpiece of understatement: "He fasted for forty days and forty
nights, and afterwards he was hungry." I should hope so.

Imagine, then, how vulnerable he must have been when the
devil came along and invited him to take control of the situation
and turn stones into bread. How easy to escape the anxiety and
pain of the wilderness.

Jesus said "No!" Instead, he risked his life and his ministry on
the conviction that God was in control and that God could be
trusted.

Indeed, all three of the temptations were invitations to escape
from the wilderness, to take control, and to create a life that was
predictable and safe.

Instead Jesus remained in this scary, unpredictable world and

trusted God one day at a time, which is no mean task—especially
when you find yourself hanging from a cross.

The good news of the Gospel is not that God can help us escape from the wilderness. The good news is that by the grace of
God we can learn to be at home in the wilderness.

*Learning to be at home in the wilderness is essential to our ca-
pacity to say "goodbye."*

Our quest for "civilization" is above all a quest for security. Ultimately the obsession with security is an obsession with death. That
is what Jesus meant when he said "Whosoever seeks their life will
lose it." Our fear of death cripples our ability to undertake the risks
of living in the wilderness of this chaotic and fallen world.

I know a young black woman who belonged to a predominantly
white congregation. She married a black professor at the local university. The service was at the church, and the whole congregation
came. Everyone rejoiced for Margee and Joe.

But Margee and Joe knew one thing that no one else knew. Joe
suffered from sickle cell anemia—a disease that peculiarly afflicts
black people and is ultimately fatal.

Margee and Joe did not know whether they would have two
weeks or two months or two years together. They celebrated their
anniversaries each month ..." monthiversaries."

As it turned out they had two years together. Then one day Joe
came home from school not feeling well. Twenty-four hours later
he was gone.

Shortly afterwards I saw Margee and was upset by the news. She
ended up consoling me. "Look at it this way, Ed," she said with a
gentle smile, "The heavenly choirs have just gotten a great new
baritone."

*Margee knew how to be at home in the wilderness, and there-
fore she knew how to say "goodbye."*

Recently I was doing a retreat with the pastor and governing
board (Session) of a Presbyterian Church. We were involved in a
deep discussion of what it meant for the Session to exercise "spiritual oversight of the flock."

Suddenly an older woman burst into tears. "I don't understand
this conversation," she said. "Five years ago when my husband died,
none of you came to see me! The only person who came to see me
was the pastor. I had known all of you for years. I kept coming to
church. But none of you came to see me!"

She became so upset that she had to leave the room. The Session sat in stunned silence. Finally, we had a season of prayer.

About twenty minutes later the woman came back. She had re-
covered her composure. It was "confession time."

"I knew how much you were hurting," said one Elder. "And I wanted so much to come and see you. But I was afraid. I was afraid I'd say the wrong thing."

Another Elder said, "I was afraid I wouldn't know what to say."

Of course her reply was, "You wouldn't have had to say anything at all. All you had to do was be there."

But you see, they were afraid to be there because they had not learned how to be at home in the wilderness. Thus they were afraid to be with her when the wilderness invaded her life.

How do we learn to be at home in the wilderness?

I knew a fine young pastor who was tall, handsome, and athletic. He had a beautiful wife and a fine congregation.

At age 34 he learned that he had Hodgkin's disease. For the next six years he carried on a courageous struggle that included several rounds of chemotherapy.

In response to the first round he got better and was back in the pulpit. Then the disease returned and the chemotherapy this time destroyed his hips. Twice within six months he had to undergo major operations to replace his hip sockets. The second time he almost died from an infection.

Again he was back in the pulpit. But the disease was persistent and eventually the time came when it was evident that the chemotherapy would no longer arrest the cancer. He grew thinner and weaker. Never have I seen anyone suffer so much for so long.

During the last weeks he and his wife spent long hours reading the psalms together. At a crucial point the psalms that meant the most were those we seldom read in church. Psalm 88, for example, is an expression of sheer despair. It was only after days of living with the psalms of despair that Dick was able to come up out of the valley of the shadow and say with conviction:

The Lord is my shepherd. ... Yea, though I walk through the valley of the shadow of death I will fear no evil (Psalm 23).

Dick and Sandy had learned how to be at home in the wilderness. Indeed, during his last days he ministered to the doctors and nurses, helping them overcome their fear of his death. By now he was badly disfigured, and when they entered his room they were afraid to look at him. He was able to help them learn that he was still there, and that they need not be afraid.

When he died, Dick had learned how to say goodbye. And we, if we are going to learn to say goodbye, must learn to trust God in the wilderness. Then we will be able to say goodbye, knowing that God is in control of our lives, and that God can be trusted.

There is a hymn specially written for those who are learning to be at home in the wilderness. It goes like this:

> Guide me, O Thou great Jehovah,
> Pilgrim through this barren land.
> I am weak, but Thou art mighty;
> Hold me with Thy powerful hand.
> Bread of heaven, bread of heaven,
> Feed me 'til I want no more,
> Feed me 'til I want no more.

NOTES

1. Tom Jones, "Never Say No," *The Fantasticks* (Hollywood, CA: MGM Records, 1960).

2. Tom Jones, "Plant a Radish," Ibid.

What to Do until the Preacher Comes: A Sermon for the Transition Time in the Life of a Congregation

by Edward A. White

> There are many parts, but one body ... if one member suffers, we all suffer together; if one member is honored, we all rejoice together. ... Now you are the Body of Christ! (1st Corinthians 12:12-27)

It is always traumatic when the pastor leaves. As the Scripture notes, we are all interdependent members of the Body of Christ. The pastor plays a sensitive role in the life of the congregation and is often with us at the most critical moments in our lives. When the pastor leaves, people feel it.

It has often been noted that in the Chinese language, the word "crisis" means both *danger* and *opportunity*. When the pastor leaves it marks the beginning of a critical transition in the life of the congregation. Transitions can be the greatest periods of growth for an individual or a community. If growth occurs in a congregation during the period between installed pastors, it can mean new opportunity in the next pastorate. If the tasks of the interim period are not addressed, however, the congregation can indeed be in danger.

There are *three major tasks* that confront the congregation when a pastor leaves. All of them have to do with trusting God.

I. Will You Learn to Trust God with Your Past?

This means dealing with feelings. Pastors engender strong feelings in people, and when the pastor leaves, people feel it.

Sometimes people feel anger: "How could the pastor abandon us like this?"

Sometimes people feel guilt: "What did we do that made the pastor want to go away?"

Most commonly people feel grief: "How painful it is to lose someone we trust so deeply."

Now there are no such things as right or wrong feelings. What you feel is what you feel. *The issue is whether you can own your feelings and work through them to the point where you can let go.* Only then will you be able to enter wholeheartedly into a new relationship with a new pastor. Otherwise your unresolved feelings about the former pastor will contaminate your relationship with the next one. *When we are unable to let go of the past we get stuck in history!*

In Charles Dickens' *Great Expectations* there is a character named Miss Havisham. As a young woman, Miss Havisham was to have gotten married. On her wedding day, however, the groom never came. We meet Miss Havisham twenty years later. She is still wearing her wedding dress and the wedding cake is still on the table in her mansion. Now the cake is covered with dust and infested with mice, of course. Because Miss Havisham never dealt with her feelings about her aborted wedding, she got stuck in history. She drew the curtains on her life and became a stifling influence on those around her.

I know a large congregation where every year during Lent they have "home communions" in which groups of twenty people gather in homes for Bible study, a communion service, and fellowship. Because the congregation is large, there are more communions than the pastors can cover, so I have often been asked to lead one or two.

One year I went to a home and met with twenty-two people, all in their seventies and all of whom had belonged to the church for thirty-five or forty years. We had a pleasant evening of Bible study and Communion. But all evening long the folks talked about dear old Dr. So-and-So and how he had been ill recently in the hospital but was now home again. Had I been a stranger I would have assumed from the conversation that Dr. So-and-So must be the pastor of the congregation. In fact, Dr. So-and-So had retired as pastor twenty years before!

I felt as if I were in a whole room full of Miss Havishams.

Next day I visited the current pastor of the congregation and reviewed the names of these twenty-two people. Sure enough, only two of them were regular current participants in the life of the church. The rest sent in their annual pledge, and perhaps came at Easter.

But for all practical purposes, their active life in the Body of Christ ended twenty years ago. They got stuck in history because they never dealt with their feelings about the loss of their former pastor. They never learned to trust God with their past!

Elisabeth Kubler-Ross, in her book *On Death and Dying*,[1] notes five stages in the grief process: 1) Denial, 2) Depression, 3) Bargaining, 4) Despair, and 5) Acceptance. The members of the congregation must make their spiritual journey through these stages to let go of a relationship that is now finished and prepare themselves for a new relationship with the next pastor.

Trusting God with the past also means being open to learn from the experiences of the past. Before the past becomes too much an idealized memory it is well to undertake some critical review of the congregation's story. What can be learned about the values, meanings, and priorities of this particular church? Are there some patterns of behavior that have been dysfunctional? Are there unresolved issues we need to face to get our house in order before the next pastor comes? Are there reconciliations that need to occur among members or groups within the congregation?

II. Will You Learn to Trust God with Your Present?

Over time, congregations often become overly dependent on the pastor, especially in a long pastorate. Folks tend to become spectators, who come to cheer the superstar in the pulpit on Sunday morning who is *The Minister*.

When a vacuum is created by the departure of the pastor, sometimes people are moved to step forward and assume responsibility. The congregation suddenly discovers all kinds of gifts and talents of which it was unaware because these gifts were not being exercised.

The Rev. James R. Adams is the effective rector of St. Mark's Episcopal Church on Capitol Hill in Washington, D.C. After a number of years, the congregation gave Jim a sabbatical to study in England. While he was gone, they discovered many dimensions of ministry that he had been doing which they could do equally well and that should rightly be part of the people's job description. When Jim returned the folks sent him two messages: 1) "There are many things that you used to do for us that we don't want you to do any more. They are part of our ministry." 2) "There are certain things we really need you to do and do well, such as the conduct of worship and preaching. We have discovered that we need someone at the heart of the congregation for whom the congregation is at the heart of their life."

Both Jim's ministry and that of his people have been richer and more rewarding since that discovery.

The body of Christ includes all its members and needs the gifts and ministry of all its members.

As a child I grew up near Boston, which means that I was an ardent Red Sox baseball fan and an even more ardent Celtics basketball fan.

Being a Red Sox fan was the most frustrating thing in the world. They had half the stars in the American league. But in spite of all that talent, they seldom won a championship because they never learned to work together as a team. They were a bunch of individual glory boys, each trying to hit the ball out of the park. They didn't know about the squeeze bunt or the double steal.

Consequently, they often lost the tight one-run games that would have made the difference.

The Boston Celtics were just the opposite. They won the NBA Championship eleven years out of thirteen. Yet most years none of the top individual scorers were Celtics. They had such a beautifully balanced and blended team, however, that they were able to beat all the teams with the individual stars.

How can the congregation learn to function like the Celtics and not like the Red Sox? There is no better time to learn than during the interim period when the "superstar in the pulpit" isn't there.

In ministry, as in basketball, leadership is best when it is shared. Leadership is not synonymous with standing in front of the group and throwing your weight around. Leadership is the performance of any function that enables the congregation to move forward together.

I learned this lesson rather dramatically years ago in a human relations lab. Fifteen of us clergy were together in a "t-group" for ten days.

We got to know each other pretty well in that time. There was a lot of learning.

Near the end of the ten days, the trainer did a rather startling thing. He said, "I want you preachers to go line yourselves and each other up along the wall in the order of your importance in this group. I want the most important person at that end of the line and the least important at the other end. After everyone has taken their place, if you think anyone has stood in the wrong place, you are welcome to move them."

I went over and stood more or less in the middle. I didn't want to appear too arrogant. Then people began to move others around in the line. When all of the shuffling had ceased, I looked up and, behold, I was almost at the bottom of the line.

That was a good lesson in humility, but the real lesson came afterwards. The trainer than took the top half of the line (the supposedly important people) and put them in a circle in the center of the room. The rest of us sat outside and watched. The trainer gave the inner circle a task, which was to come to consensus on a particularly controversial statement.

Now each of these important people entered the circle thinking, "I'm an important person in this group, and I must not allow myself to be visibly influenced by anyone else or I shall lose face."

The result was that they cancelled each other out entirely and could get nowhere as a group.

Later, those of us from the bottom half of the line were put in a circle at the center. We all entered thinking, "We need each other. Perhaps we had better listen to and support each other."

And that is precisely how we worked. We made an excellent team as we shared the functions of leadership and drew forth the talents of everyone. We were playing the game like the Celtics.

"You are the Body of Christ, and individually members of it" (Romans 12:27). What happens to one of us affects all of us. We are called to bear one another's burdens and to share one another's joys. Trust God with your present!

III. Will You Trust God With Your Future?

You have more freedom now to determine together where you want to go from here and who you aspire to become than at any other time in your life together!

Once a new preacher comes to this church, the personality of that preacher, the strengths and weaknesses of that preacher, the theology of that preacher will have a lot to do with where you go from here, whether you want it to or not.

Now is the time for you as a congregation to take the time to think through together what your priorities are for the next chapter in the life of this church, so that you can then seek pastoral leadership that matches that vision. Scripture says, "Where there is no vision the people perish" (Proverbs 29:18). That vision needs to emerge from your community of faith and not simply be laid on you by the next pastor.

Now is the time for the congregation to wrestle with questions such as:

1. What matters most to us about our church? What keeps us coming here?

2. What would we like to change or improve?

3. What's missing?

4. What are the trends in our community that may affect our fu-

ture? Who are the potential target constituencies in our community that we can serve best? What are their needs?

5. What is our primary task? Is it to generate membership growth? To generate more and different church programs? To change society and pursue justice? To stimulate growth in discipleship and faithfulness among our church members?

Think back over the life of this congregation since you joined it. When was the Golden Age in the life of this church? Was it five years ago? Ten? Twenty?

Actually, if you think that the Golden Age is any time other than now, I will worry about you. Now is the moment that God has entrusted to you. Walter Brueggemann says, "What God does first and best and most is to trust people with their moment in history."

Can you learn to trust God with your future?

In northern Minnesota, a farmer's five-year-old child was playing in the kitchen while his mother was busily engaged in domestic chores. Unnoticed, the child toddled out of the house and into the wheat field. Shortly thereafter, noticing the child's absence, the mother began a frantic search for her baby. When she could not find the child in the immediate vicinity of the farmhouse, she called her husband, and together they searched through the heaped-up sheaves of wheat. In desperation they summoned all the farmhands. Several hours later, when the child still had not been found, the townspeople were called in. Those of every vocation, economic level, and religious faith—the minister and the rabbi, the workers and the mill owner—beat at the sheaves of wheat, walking and running in every direction, urged on by the entreaties of the father and mother.

When this proved futile, someone suggested: "We seem to be going off in all directions. Why don't we join hands, form one large circle, spread out and close in, encompassing every inch of the land?"

As a result, the preacher joined hands with the worker, and the physician joined hands with the town idler. People of every station of life and every faith joined hands to form a gigantic circle. Carefully examining every inch of the land, they narrowed the circle until someone reached down, picked up the child, and handed him to his father.

As soon as he touched the child, the father knew that his son was dead. He lifted the tiny, lifeless body in his arms and cried out, "O my God, why didn't we all join hands before it was too late."[2]

This is the time for your congregation to all join hands and reaffirm that you are one Body in Christ.

Together you can trust God with your past. You can learn from it and then let go of it.

Together you can trust God with your present. You can discover how to develop and exercise the gifts of everyone as you learn to share leadership.

Together you can trust God with your future. Share your hopes and fears and dreams. God will give you a vision of your ministry together if you ask for it.

The end of one pastorate and the beginning of another is an experience of death and resurrection. And like the first resurrection, the promise is that of new life.

Let us pray: O Lord, help us not to get stuck in history. We offer to you our grief, ourselves, and our hopes, and we pray that you will indeed take us and melt us and mold us and fill us that our life together will reflect the saving love of Jesus Christ. Amen.

NOTES

1. Elisabeth Kubler-Ross, *On Death and Dying* (New York: Macmillan Publishing Co., Inc., 1969).

2. From a sermon by William Sloane Coffin, preached March 11, 1984.

PART VII

What Are the Ethics of the Relationship after We've Said Goodbye?

In twenty-one years with National Capital Presbytery I can recall countless cases where a former pastor became a problem. The problem took many forms:

1. Returning uninvited to perform weddings, funerals, or baptisms.

2. Continuing to make pastoral visits on members of the congregation.

3. Criticizing the successor pastor to members of the congregation, or becoming the confidant of those who wished to express criticism.

4. Sometimes the former pastor chose to put the successor on the spot: "I'll be delighted to come back and do your wedding if the present pastor agrees."What is the new pastor to say when the parishioner asks if "Dear old Dr. So-and-So can come back to marry our daughter"? The former pastor should either simply say "No," or else call the incumbent himself or herself.

The underlying problem was always the same. The former pastor did not realize that "goodbye" means "goodbye" in terms of the pastoral role. It is an issue of professional ethics to recognize that the currently installed pastor of the church is precisely that, and to undermine that person's ministry is a betrayal of one's ordination vows. Ralph Johnson puts the case succinctly in his letter "From the Pastor's Desk."

Joan Mabon has dealt with this problem more than once as a professional interim pastor. In "My Friend the Former Pastor" she describes the destructive effects of continued pastoral contact with the congregation on the part of the former pastor.

In "Leaving the Pastorate: Staying in Town" Rod Reinecke describes the contract he developed with the Vestry of his congregation to ensure that his continued presence in the community would not become a problem. He learned that a clear written contract is not enough.

In "Dear Henry" John Esau describes the standards he followed when remaining in a congregation after ceasing to be its pastor. He concludes that "in order to make the relationship work, I must do things right, the congregation must respond appropriately to me and the new pastor must feel positive about it. If any one of these three does not work, it is clear that it is inappropriate to stay in a former congregation."

It is not necessary, and perhaps not even healthy, for the former pastor to sever all *personal* ties in the congregation. The critical issue is the distinction between personal friendships and *being in the role of the pastor*.

Rabbi Edwin Friedman, in his book *Generation to Generation*[1], suggests that the "lame duck period" in a pastorate can be an unusual time of emotional growth for both pastor and congregation if the pastor exercises appropriate leadership. He recommends four elements in a separation strategy:

1. When folks react to your decision to leave, don't react back. Respond, but don't react.

2. Allow the other parties to react. They need to work through and let go of their feelings to get on with their future.

3. Be a nonanxious part of the transition process, but don't be involved in the selection of a successor. "Exit interviews" can be mutually helpful to pastor and lay leaders.

4. Staying in touch after the separation without getting "triangled" into ongoing congregational issues. The role of "friend and former pastor" can often be affirmed by returning on invitation to participate in special celebrations such as "homecoming Sunday" or an anniversary. Often a healthy friendship can develop between past and present pastor, especially when the latter is clear that the former is genuinely supportive of his or her ministry.

NOTE

1. Edwin H. Friedman, *Generation to Generation* (New York: The Guilford Press, 1985).

From the Pastor's Desk

by Ralph Johnson

One of the hardest elements of a dissolution of a pastoral relationship, for both the members of the congregation and the pastor, is the necessity to *really* terminate the asking for or the offer of professional services. It's especially true in the case of weddings, funerals, baptisms, hospital calls, or counselling. Because such occasions have been so integral a part of our close association over the years, it's very tempting to assume that there would be no harm for me, if asked, to come back to perform them again.

But long experience in countless congregations declares otherwise. Real damage is done when former pastors return to perform such services because it serves to delay, confuse, or even undermine the bonding that should rightfully occur between the members of the congregation and the new pastor.

I am sure you will agree with me that forming a good, strong relationship with your future pastor deserves the very best each of us can offer. And that "best" surely includes a commitment from you and me not to ask for, nor to offer such services.

How grateful I am that our faith makes it possible for us to accept such a closure with *positive* feelings! For after all, we are but the "actors" in this grand drama of God's redemption. And even though we come on stage or leave, the Author abides unchanged and eternal! That's really all that matters.

My Friend, the Former Pastor

by Joan Mabon

When the pastor leaves a congregation, many people there feel they have lost a trusted friend. Like the eternal presence of God, the presence of God's ministers takes on an aura of permanence, and we are surprised and hurt when the relationship must end. The break is as hard for the pastor as for the congregation. When trials and joys have been deeply shared, meaningful bonds develop.

The difficulty comes as both pastor and members shift roles. The pastor ceases to be pastor/friend and becomes friend only; members cease being associates/clients/advocates/friends and also become friends only.

Relationships must then be redefined as friendships alone, apart from the ecclesiastical roles. The depth of mutual loss and grief is often so great that the inherent difficulty in shifting these roles and redefining those relationships becomes compounded by mutual pain.

But shifted and redefined they must be, and the more intentionally and clearly those role shifts are made, the sooner the pastor and members alike can establish healthy new church relationships.

Interim work keeps me continually in touch with persons who are grieving for a lost relationship. And I am continually surprised by the difficulty pastors and members clearly experience in terminating relationships.

In every congregation I have known or studied, members and pastors consistently seek and give friendly concern, sympathy, visits, cards, letters, bulletins, hospital calls, sacramental services, taped sermons, and recommendations on the succeeding pastor. The difficulty in ending all of that is not surprising. The grief itself is not surprising. What is surprising is the quantity and persistence of continuing contacts that represent a futile struggle to "hang on."

These contacts occur very often in a covert way, as though it's not OK for new leaders to know about them. They occur very often under the guise of "friendship," even though the previous relationship may have been distant. During the painful confusion of terminating and shifting roles, contacts of all sorts and kinds continue indefinitely until someone asks, "How is this contact maturing my faith? How is it building up the community where I have chosen to witness?"

Congregational members and departed pastors seem to feel that continuing contacts are private matters "just between old friends." A member in contact with a former pastor, however, generally focuses individually on that relationship and is unable to see how maintaining that tie affects other members or impedes their relationship with a new pastor. A departed pastor, away from the scene, is unable to perceive the overall implications for the whole congregation.

Because we are truly "members one of another," however, even a few contacts do have an effect on the total congregation. Repeated interactions have a rippling effect and can stimulate profound waves of reaction.

From the vantage point of leadership within grieving congregations, I have listed some effects I perceive from the former pastor's continuing relationship.

Ten Effects a Departed Pastor's Continuing Contacts Have on a Congregation:

1. Contacts continue to resurface for members whenever negative emotions were present at the pastor's departure.
    —Regret: "It's not like it used to be."
    —Inadequacy: "He left us for a better church."
    —Guilt: "Why didn't I do enough to make her stay?"
    —Anger: "Why did he leave us flat?"
    —Loneliness: "I miss her."
    —Frustration: "If he were here I could cope."
    —Relief: "I'm glad he's gone and we don't have to do *that* anymore!"

2. Contacts deny members the opportunity to work through those emotions of grief directly and constructively, and encourage their futile grappling with ghosts.

3. Contacts discourage members' working through their feelings within the community ("I'd better not tell my Deacon that I called

the old pastor") and encourage a rivalry among members ("The pastor called *me!*")

4. Private contacts with individuals deprive the community of the opportunity to share grief and loneliness, to build the strength that comes from shared suffering, to discover resurrected hope that emerges from shared struggles.

5. Contacts focus members' energy outside the congregation at a time when that energy may be needed most within the community.

6. Private communications encourage "holding on" to the past and fighting former battles—this time with the invisible contenders; they decrease a person's ability to struggle with present realities and diminish hope for the future.

7. Contacts confuse persons as to where and how to direct their commitment to new leadership; they make that difficult task even more difficult for members.

8. Each contact places the resident pastor in the awkward position of interloper. Interim specialists are trained to deal with the negativism so that the installed pastor can begin positive building at the earliest opportunity.

9. By surfacing implicit comparisons between new and old, contacts undermine the choice of a new pastor and inhibit a whole-hearted commitment to the new relationship.

10. Contacts keep the new pastor on the defensive and subvert that pastor's morale and effectiveness. The new pastor can never successfully compete with the old pastor's enshrined "ghost" so long as that ghost is actively present.

Leaving the Pastorate: Staying in Town

by Rod Reinecke

How can churches prevent conflict when former pastors remain in the same community? In recent years, more clergy have been buying their own homes. Some remain there when they retire, while others move from their pastorates into new forms of ministry in the area. Here is one approach involving the use of a written agreement at the time of separating.

I've sometimes thought that the saga of the almost 16-year relationship between me and my last congregation might be entitled, "And Lived to Tell the Story!"

Together, the Church of the Holy Comforter in Burlington, North Carolina and I had gone through my marital separation, divorce, solo parenthood, and eventual courtship and remarriage. Several years later I decided to leave that position, but to remain in the same town in a different role. After twenty-five years in pastorates, I would focus my full-time ministry doing marriage and family therapy and as a consultant, especially with church systems.

Yet I knew from my previous consulting experience that having a former pastor or rector around was fraught with possible difficulties. Cliques could form. Some parishioners might fail to recognize and accept the change in leadership. The former pastor or rector could easily become inappropriately involved in the life of the parish, or in the lives of parishioners. Other clergy who were potential candidates in the search process might be very wary of accepting such a call. How might such conflicts be avoided?

I remembered the letter of agreement the Vestry and I had formulated in the past, prior to a sabbatical I had taken. And I also remembered an agreement for separating that I had seen in the mid-Lent, 1978 issue of "Leaven," the newsletter of the National Network of Episcopal Clergy Associations. Both processes had seemed to clarify mutual expectations, although that "separation agreement" I had seen came out of an unhappy and "involuntary" termination.

I decided to propose a written agreement for separating and negotiate that with the Vestry, making it available to the congregation so that all would be familiar with it. The Vestry concurred, and the final agreement is reproduced at the conclusion of this article.

In a letter to the congregation in 1983, I wrote:

> It will be important for me to 'clear the way' for a new rector and to give time and space for a period of adjustment and the calling, coming, and establishment of that new leader. He or she must be unhampered by me and the long relationship we have had. I am determined to 'hear, see, and speak no evil' about any Interim (priest) or eventually called clergy. I have asked the Vestry to join me in working out and publishing an agreement about my future relationship with the Parish.

What follows is how that written agreement seems to have helped or hindered in our separation, in the transition, and eventually with a new rector. Through the Rector, copies of this article were made available to interested members of the congregation for their anonymous comments.

I believed that publicizing the agreement would help in the process of explaining to parishioners that I would decline various pastoral activities, including officiating or even assisting at baptisms, funerals, and weddings. Unfortunately, once again I learned that publishing information in letters, newsletters, or bulletins does not mean that one has communicated.

There were inevitably some who had not seen or noticed this material for one reason or another. So there were a few requests, but I referred them all to the Interim Priest or the Rector as the appropriate liturgical and pastoral representative of the Parish or Bishop. I followed this practice also with nonEpiscopalian friends or clients in the community.

The rationale for the agreement was published separately in newsletters and bulletin messages. Exactly why I would decline ongoing pastoral involvement was therefore missed by some parishioners. In fact, a few of these apparently misunderstood and indignantly thought the Vestry was forcing this agreement on me. Still others seemed to think I was leaving the ministry altogether. Such misapprehensions seem to have been cleared up in chance meetings I had with those in the community who asked about these things.

My hope was that a clear and well-publicized written agreement would also make it possible for my wife and me to return eventually to the parish in new roles as worshippers. We realized this would take time and care. Meanwhile, my stepdaughter—the only one of our offspring still at home—decided she would continue to worship and participate there while we visited elsewhere.

My wife, Ruth Wright, and I found several things about the transition time difficult. For about a year and a half, we had no regular place of worship and belonging, although we were welcomed warmly at a new Episcopal congregation in nearby Greensboro. Our consulting and training work took us out of town often on weekends, so we worshipped in many places. It was educational to see what was happening in other churches, but left us feeling rather rootless—a situation that continued because of our periodic weekend work.

For me, the most difficult aspects of leaving the parish and staying in town were being separated for some time from our major local source of support, plus not feeling free to call on former parishioners in their times of need. Another hard choice was whether to attend weddings or funerals of friends in the parish before the new rector was fully settled.

Our return to the parish was low key. We started coming to the early Sunday morning service after there had been an interim priest for a year, and following several months of ministry with their new Rector, David R. Williams. Ruth and I had known him previously.

We decided not to attend any parish functions where the new Rector would be present for the first time (such as annual events like a parish meeting, picnic, progressive dinner, etc.), so as to let him and his family enjoy these without distraction. He was sensitive to our desires to protect the parish and ourselves from inappropriate involvements, but he was also interested in exploring more positive potential in the relationship.

He was also conscious of my need to make a living and to keep up with my scheduled clients during the week and often on weekends away. I had been sensitive to the fact that I was the only other resident Episcopal priest in the county. If emergencies developed that required an ordained person and he was away, what alternatives might there be?

The Rector and Vestry established and published an arrangement for meeting pastoral needs in his absence through a system including a) an "on call" person (dispatcher); b) a pastoral calling committee; c) professional lay pastors (trained counselors who are also members of the Parish); d) a priest. This system could call on clergy in adjoining counties who would be reimbursed for any professional services offered. This left the congregation and me free of any obligatory involvement, but might pave the way for new possibilities in the future.

We will explore those possibilities as time goes by and more and more parishioners feel comfortable with the changes that have occurred. Meanwhile, a new relationship continues to develop and our hope is that this process will prove useful to others elsewhere. The following Letter of Agreement seems to have played a helpful role. It was also adapted more recently as an agreement between the Rev. Keith John Reeve and St. Mark's Episcopal Church, Raleigh, North Carolina. It proved useful as that Rector left after seventeen years there to begin a new ministry serving as an Interim Pastor, while maintaining his home in Raleigh. We served as consultants to the Reeves during their transition and are grateful for their added insights.

Letter of Agreement

This is a Letter of Agreement at the time of separation between Rod Reinecke and the Vestry of the Church of the Holy Comforter, Burlington, North Carolina. It is the result of a process of clarification of the former rector's role as he continues to live in the area.

It is to be shared throughout the congregation so that others may understand changes in role and responsibilities and can cooperate together as the parish and former rector move into another phase of their respective lives.

1. The Rector's resignation, effective January 1, 1984, signifies his understanding that all priestly, pastoral, and administrative duties in this Parish are terminated as of that date.

2. It is further mutually understood that this applies also to the interim period before another rector is called, since the congregation needs some time and space between rectors to discover who they are now, where they want to go, and with what new leadership. It is agreed that the Vestry will make provision for other interim pastoral and priestly ministry for the congregation.

3. The former rector agrees that he will not officiate or assist at any baptism, wedding, or funeral in this Parish, but may attend as a worshipper on occasion. He expects to exercise his ministry in other parishes as invited. This will prevent divided loyalties in the congregation and pressures on either the former or future rectors or interim priests.

4. The former rector agrees further that if attending this Parish in the future, it will be as a worshipper and participant, and that he will neither say nor listen to any uncomplimentary or critical re-

marks concerning the interim clergy, past or future rectors in social or other gatherings.

5. It is agreed that the former rector will be independent of the church office and staff.

6. If, after a suitable period of time, there is a desire on the part of the next rector to review any of the above items, he or she may instigate that with the consent of the Vestry and provided the former rector is willing for such review and renegotiation to occur.

7. The Rector's Discretionary Fund is to be transferred back to the Parish to be held for the new rector or used at the discretion of the Vestry.

8. The former rector will remove his own vestments, equipment, books, and possessions by December 31, 1983. Items he has used, belonging to the Parish, have been inventoried and will remain there. Keys to the parish rooms and buildings will be returned by him to the Wardens symbolically at the evening service on December 18.

Date   Senior Warden

               Junior Warden

               Former Rector

Dear Henry

by John A. Esau

Dear Henry,

I am responding to your letter in which you raise the question
about the outgoing pastor and his relationship to the congregation
that he has pastored.

As you know, it is a key question for me because I have also
chosen to remain in the congregation where I was pastor. I am well
aware of the fact that this is against the larger wisdom of past experience, and yet I feel that it has been a good and workable choice
in our case.

Having said that, I should quickly add that the persons to ask
are not me but the current pastoral team, and they should be asked
that in settings where they feel no pressure to answer any way but
honestly. I do know of situations where the former pastor had felt
good about the relationship, while the current pastor perceived it
quite differently, and not positively.

I think, nevertheless, that I have learned something out of my
own experience that has been helpful. First of all, before leaving
the congregation I indicated my intent and the rules by which I intended to live following the termination of my ministry. I told the
congregation on a Sunday morning that I would not respond to any
requests for funerals or weddings or any acts of public ministry.
This was tested a couple of times, and when it became clear that I
meant that and held to that, evidently the rest of the congregation
caught on, and now the issue is no longer pursued.

I found the greatest test when a woman of our congregation
called our home to report she had a reoccurrence of cancer. I was
not home at the time, fortunately, and my wife answered the phone.
I called our pastor and her response was also helpful; she said to
me, "Thank you. I will respond to her." In that situation I did not

even return the phone call to the person who called me; and then, of course, I had to deal with my own conscience. I am still convinced that my response was right.

I also indicated to the congregation my intent not to participate in leadership roles in the congregation for some time to come. After three years, I am still maintaining that position. I did agree to several minor short-term tasks, and found even those complicated and compromised my basic stance.

What that means, of course, is that I sacrifice my right to be a normal member of the congregation, and if I could not live with that, I should see it as my obligation to move elsewhere. I further picked up along the way that former pastors should not attend congregational meetings. Again, I have basically held to that, with one exception, and I was sorry in that case to be there. When some comments were made, I looked for doors of escape, but saw only windows and knew that I was caught in a very awkward moment.

Another element that I believe former pastors must sacrifice to remain in their former congregation is that they must give up the normal right to be critical about anything. I am not talking about the supercritics, but about the normal right that all of us have to evaluate people and events. As a former pastor it is only my right to affirm, and happily for me that has been easy with our new pastoral team. Obviously within the sanctuary of our home, from time to time, I voice some subdued complaints to my wife, who has always been better at keeping those things quiet than I have.

I have also tried to maintain contact and openness with our present pastor, and believe that we have the kind of relationship that is free to be honest with each other. It has felt good on a couple of occasions when he has sought my counsel, but I have tried very hard not to offer counsel when it was not asked.

Finally, there is a very subtle issue that I have not always found easy, and that is how to respond to people simply in meeting them either at church or elsewhere. It is very easy to fall back into a pastoral attitude, and for a time I had simply to withdraw myself as quickly as possible from public meetings and worship. But now it feels much better in meeting them as brothers and sisters who are a part of this congregation.

I trust that these comments will be helpful to you. I am glad that others are taking the issue seriously, and I hope that we can learn from one another. While many of us have challenged the tradition that it is best to move elsewhere, I guess my best sense is that there is still wisdom in that counsel.

I have said that to make the relationship work, I must do things right, the congregation must respond appropriately to me, and the new pastor must feel positive about it. If any one of those three does not work, it is clear that it is inappropriate to stay in a former congregation.

Sincerely,
John A. Esau

PART VIII

Conclusion: Learning to Live with Risk and Uncertainty

A friend of mine has a t-shirt that reads: LIFE IS A TEMPORARY AS-SIGNMENT.

Meister Eckhart, the twelfth century mystic, said that in the course of life we travel four spiritual paths:

1. *The Positive Way:* The path that leads us to awe and wonder and an appreciation of creation. This path is grounded in the Incarnation of Jesus Christ, God's ultimate affirmation of creation.

2. *The Negative Way:* The path that teaches us how to let go of possessions, loved ones, health, and ultimately even life itself. This is the path on which we encounter suffering, loss, and grief. It is also the path on which we give up possessions and illusions about ourselves. This path is grounded in the Cross, which was Jesus' ultimate act of letting go.

3. *The Creative Way:* Wherein we discover that God has given us gifts to discover, develop, and use. In the words of Matthew Fox, "Beauty is born of the coupling of love of life and its harmonies with pain at life and its discords." This path is grounded in the Resurrection with its promise of new life.

4. *The Transforming Way:* The path that leads us to commit our lives to compassion and justice which is the Will of God. This path is grounded in the coming of the Holy Spirit. "Being able to rejoice at another person's happiness is like being in heaven."

For most people I suspect that the second path, the Negative Way, is the most formidable. We do not like to give up roles that are important to us, nor relationships that mean a lot. We do not like the experience of death.

And yet the Negative Way is the key to unlocking the succeeding paths. We must learn to let go and trust God to discover, develop, and exercise our creative gifts. Only as we learn to live with pain and loss can we truly have compassion for ("a feeling with") the pain and loss of others.

Roy Oswald has suggested that the manner in which we terminate relationships with friends and parishioners when leaving a parish can be a precursor of the way in which we will face death.

Oswald also notes that when the pastor says goodbye there are five termination tasks, four of which are similar to the tasks confronting a person near the end of life. I experienced these tasks in the process of leaving National Capital Presbytery after almost twenty-two years:

1. *The Need to Take Control of What Remains of "This Life"*

The pastor needs to be intentional in using the time between announcing the resignation and actual departure to bring closure with the various individuals and groups in the congregation. Some need a visit, others a letter, still others a phone call.

This "closure" is important for both pastor and people so that they will experience resolution of this chapter in their life together to be emotionally and spiritually free to enter wholeheartedly into their separate futures.

When I left the Presbytery Executive position there were six major farewell parties involving different constituencies in the Presbytery. I wrote over a hundred letters and received twice that many. There were numerous lunches with key friends including members of the Presbytery staff. Saying goodbye was an almost full-time job that involved the better part of two months. We were able to celebrate and be thankful for all the times and meanings we had shared together. As a result I believe the Presbytery and I were enabled to enter into our subsequent separate journeys without the "encumbrance of incompleteness." We were able to say joyfully together "It Is Finished" in order that each might be able to begin again.

2. *The Need to Get Our Affairs in Order*

Our responsibilities must be turned over to others so that the life of the community of faith can continue decently and in order. In the closing weeks I found myself systematically turning over files, history, and assignments to various Presbytery staff and leaders. This was a key part of the experience of letting go, to actually turn over piece by piece the responsibilities I had carried to specific people who would now assume them. By the time of my departure I occupied a position that no longer had functions to perform.

3. *The Need to Let Old Grudges Go*
After announcing my resignation I was visited by several people with whom I had had altercations at one time or another. They anxiously asked if these problems had influenced my decision to resign. Happily, I could reassure them that this was not so. We then had a good conversation about our differences which brought healing.

Rabbi Edwin Friedman points out that extreme emotional reactivity is an indication of a failure to separate. "The most intense forms of reactivity in marital divorce—battles over property, visiting rights, support payments, etc.—are evidence that the couple has *failed to separate*. And the continuing struggle inhibits further separation."[1]

The pastor must monitor his or her own reactive behavior while making room for reactivity on the part of members of the congregation.

> The ability to allow reactivity in the other without reciprocating creates the best chance that both partners can go on to their next relationships with the least amount of emotional baggage.[2]

4. *The Need to Say "Thank You"*
I was overwhelmed by the expressions of gratitude that came from many people. I also found myself seeking out many people to thank whose love and support I had taken for granted for so many years. It's unfortunate that we so often fail to express appreciation until the end is near. But that's why it is so very important to do it then.

5. *The Need to be Straight and Clear about Reasons for Leaving*
Nature abhors a vacuum. If you are not clear about your reasons for leaving, people will fill the vacuum with their imaginations. What they imagine will invariably be worse than the reality. They may conjure up all manner of fantasies that cause them to feel either anger or guilt.

I was fortunate to be able to tell the Presbytery that my decision to leave was not rooted in any disaffection with either the job or with people. The reasons had to do with a changing sense of call, with family needs, and with desired changes in personal lifestyle to grow old gracefully.

However, if there had been negative reasons it would have been important to share them and engage in the dialogue that would follow. Truthfulness is a prelude to healthy closure.

* * *

The contributors to this anthology have shared with us a rich variety of experience. They teach us:

1. That the pastor must exercise the initiative of discerning when it's time to leave.

2. That trusted friends at the core of the congregation's life can be a helpful source of feedback.

3. That facing a leavetaking is analogous to facing death, and the categories of Kubler-Ross can be helpful in understanding and responding to what is going on.

4. That it is essential to monitor and own our feelings each step of the way (i.e., to be in touch with our interior journey to be in touch with God).

5. That facing the crisis of departure can sometimes uncover for us unfinished business out of our own past.

6. That worship plays an important part in graceful terminations.

7. That the transition time can allow the congregation a fresh appreciation of its past and a new sense of possibility about the future.

8. That "goodbye" means "goodbye," an end to the pastoral role in that parish!

The central fact about saying goodbye is that it brings us face-to-face with ourselves and the issue of our relationship to God.

Perhaps the most powerful community of transformation that exists today is Alcoholics Anonymous. One of the essential beliefs of AA is that "the only person you can change is yourself."

In learning to be "at home in the wilderness" of a pastoral transition, we can experience in new ways what it means to trust God and to be changed in unexpected ways.

May the prayer of every clergyperson be that as they leave a parish, God will be accessible to them in such a manner that the grace of God will be communicated to the congregation in their farewell.

Sooner or later the world breaks everyone ... and then some of us become stronger at the broken places.[3]

NOTES

1. Edwin H. Friedman, *Generation to Generation* (New York: The Guilford Press, 1985), 258.

2. Ibid.

3. Attributed to Ernest Hemingway.

While You're Saying Goodbye: A Checklist of Items for a Pastor's Consideration on Leaving a Congregation

by Keith J. Reeve

The following list of considerations has been devised by the author after experiencing several Interim Pastorates and after presenting his findings to his Clergy Association and receiving helpful feedback and additional suggestions.

Although this list was specifically developed for the use of Episcopal Rectors, pastors in other denominations might find it helpful.

It is envisioned that the departing clergyperson is giving at least two months' notice so that adequate "goodbyes" may be said.

1. Agree about Your Future Relationship with the Congregation

A *written* agreement, carefully worked out with the vestry, signed by you and the senior warden (and bishop?), needs to be shared with all members of the congregation. This agreement spells out any conditions under which you will return (e.g., at the Institution of the next rector) and your availability for telephone as well as other visits.

If you decide to make commitments to any members, before you leave, to attend or participate in weddings, baptisms, funerals, etc., these commitments should be shared with the vestry and recorded in a file left for your successor. Include in your discussion your and their expectations about what will happen when someone becomes ill and is hospitalized, for example, soon after you leave.

Any promises or commitments you have made to members of the staff should also be shared with the vestry and recorded for your successor.

2. Provide an Up-to-date List of Members

Provide an up-to-the-minute list of addresses, phone numbers, (home and office), of all those who attend, regardless of their official status.

Include names and ages of children. Include birthdays, baptisms, and wedding anniversaries. Include those you have declared inactive (with notes) as well as information about those who attend but are not members.

Designate the homebound and those in nursing homes. Make a note of those who expect to be visited in their homes and the regularity of such visits. Include information about the recently bereaved, recently married, and recently divorced.

Include notes on such significant pastoral concerns as wedding plans (where are you with premarriage counseling?), pregnancies (ETA?), upcoming baptisms, divorces, retirements, etc. Indicate those who have preplanned their funerals, noting where that information is filed.

Describe parking and visitation arrangements with all local nursing homes, hospitals, etc.

Include information on those who expect confessions and home communions (specify any Lay Eucharistic Ministry arrangements) and also any arrangements you have with clergy in nearby communities for visiting your members in nursing homes, hospitals, etc., in their areas.

3. Prepare a Calendar for the Coming Year

Include dates of the bishop's next visit, "traditional services" (homecoming, patronal feasts, sunrise, graduation, etc.), canvass, congregational meetings, and any plans made for vestry or parish retreats.

Leave clear instructions about local community/ecumenical customs regarding your congregation's participation in services, programs, etc., and when it is going to be your next turn to preach or host.

4. Note All Special Funds

List the particulars of the discretionary fund, noting any special arrangements and expectations. List particulars of all other special funds to which you are privy, their purpose, use, and signatories. Include details of scholarship and other commitments you have made.

If there is a safe, where is it? Who knows the combination? If there is a bank deposit box, where is it? Who has the key?

5. Prepare Files

Make sure your parish and service registers are up-to-date and that you have signed all necessary documents. Check through the marriage entries to be sure they are in good order.

Go through your files, getting rid of unnecessary material and storing historic documents.

Prepare files containing recent annual reports, transfers recently made and those still incomplete, copies of budgets for past three years, by-laws, audits, etc.

Prepare a file of service leaflets from the past three years.

Prepare a file containing lay reader certificates, list of current members of altar guild, ushers, acolytes, etc., together with notes about how you have conducted worship and whether or not the congregation expects to be greeted at the door after the service and expectations for the coffee hour.

Include a file concerning all current arrangements for the use of the church buildings.

One file should include notes on the location of such items as the home communion set, last year's palms, the chrism, etc. Include instructions about any security devices.

Leave a set of clearly tagged keys.